Drake — Duck

Two mallards

A flock of wild geese flying south in a V shape

Here are some feathers that make up a kestrel's wing.

Baby blue tits in a tree nest

The guillemot's egg is pear-shaped

Birds

Written by Jill Bailey and David Burnie
Consultant: Ben Hoare

Senior editor Gill Pitts
Editor Olivia Stanford
Assistant editor Kritika Gupta
Editorial assistance Cécile Landau
Senior art editor Ann Cannings
Art editor Rashika Kachroo
Illustrators Abby Cook, Dan Crisp, Shahid Mahmood
Jacket co-ordinator Francesca Young
Jacket designers Dheeraj Arora, Amy Keast, Faith Nelson
DTP designers Vijay Kandwal, Dheeraj Singh

Picture researcher Sakshi Saluja
Producer, pre-production Dragana Puvacic
Producer Isabell Schart
Managing editors Soma B. Chowdhury,
Laura Gilbert, Monica Saigal
Managing art editors Neha Ahuja Chowdhry,
Diane Peyton Jones
Art director Martin Wilson
Publisher Sarah Larter
Publishing director Sophie Mitchell

Original edition
Senior editor Susan McKeever
Art editor Vicky Wharton
Editor Jodi Block
Senior art editor Jacquie Gulliver
Production Catherine Semark
Editorial consultant Peter Colston, The British Museum
(Natural History), Tring.
Illustrators Diana Catchpole, Angelika Elsebach, Jane Gedye, Nick
Hewetson, Ruth Lindsay, Louis Mackay, Polly Noakes, Lorna Turpin

First published in Great Britain in 1992.
This edition first published in Great Britain in 2017 by
Dorling Kindersley Limited
80 Strand, London, WC2R 0RL

Copyright © 1992, 1996, 2017 Dorling Kindersley Limited
A Penguin Random House Company
8 7 6 5 4 3 2 1
001–308947–Nov/2017

All rights reserved.
No part of this publication may be reproduced, stored in or introduced into a retrieval system, or transmitted,
in any form, or by any means (electronic, mechanical, photocopying, recording, or otherwise), without the prior written permission of the copyright owner.

A CIP catalogue record for this book is available from the British Library..
ISBN: 978-0-2412-8250-2

Printed and bound in China.

The publisher would like to thank the following for their kind permission to reproduce their photographs:
(Key: a-above; b-below/bottom; c-centre; f-far; l-left; r-right; t-top)

4 123RF.com: Delmas Lehman (cra). **5 iStockphoto.com**: Roger Whiteway. **7 Corbis**: Frits van Daalen / NiS / Minden Pictures (b). **8 Getty Images**: Koki Iino (cla). **13 123RF.com**: Michael Mill (tr). **17 123RF.com**: Renamarie (clb). **18 iStockphoto.com**: pum_eva (cr). **19 Alamy Stock Photo**: Nature Picture Library (cra). **Dreamstime.com**: Ajdibilio (cla). **20 Corbis**: DLILLC (b). **21 Corbis**: Tim Laman / National Geographic Creative (tr). **22 Dorling Kindersley**: Natural History Museum, London (cra). **25 123RF.com**: Anna Yakimova (tl). **27 123RF.com**: Witold Kaszkin (cla). **28 123RF.com**: Vladimir Seliverstov (br). **Dreamstime.com**: Liqiang Wang (tr). **29 123RF.com**: Michael Lane (tr). **Alamy Stock Photo**: Duncan Usher (br). **Dreamstime.com**: Barbara Zimmermann (cla). **30 123RF.com**: Juho Salo (cra). **33 123RF.com**: Dmytro Pylypenko (clb); Michael Lane (cr). **iStockphoto.com**: William Sherman (t). **34 iStockphoto.com**: Roger Whiteway (l). **35 123RF.com**: Michael Lane (cla). **36 123RF.com**: Dave Montreuil (clb). **Alamy Stock Photo**: Dave Watts (c). **38 Alamy Stock Photo**: Dave Watts (crb). **Dorling Kindersley**: The National Birds of Prey Centre, Gloucestershire (bc). **39 123RF.com**: Christian Musat (br); Jose Manuel Gelpi Diaz (t). **40 Dorling Kindersley**: British Wildlife Centre, Surrey, UK. **40-41 123RF.com**: Snike (t). **41 Dorling Kindersley**: Natural History Museum, London (cra). **42 123RF.com**: Steve Byland (clb). **Alamy Stock Photo**: Keith M Law (cra). **43 iStockphoto.com**: Paul Vinten (br). **44 123RF.com**: Delmas Lehman. **45 123RF.com**: Berka (cr). **Dreamstime.com**: Dennis Jacobsen (bl). **46 Alamy Stock Photo**: Kevin Maskell (b). **47 123RF.com**: David Tyrer (ca, crb); Ewan Chesser (clb). **Fotolia**: Gail Johnson (cr). **48 123RF.com**: Dave Montreuil (crb). **49 123RF.com**: Abi Warner (tr); Feathercollector (cla). **SuperStock**: age fotostock (b). **51 123RF.com**: Panu Ruangjan (cra); Steve Byland (br). **Alamy Stock Photo**: Wildlife GmbH (cl). **52 Getty Images**: Alice Cahill (crb). **53 Alamy Stock Photo**: Rolf Nussbaumer Photography (r). **Corbis**: Frits van Daalen / NiS / Minden Pictures (b); Otto Plantema / Buiten-beeld / Minden Pictures (cl). **54 123RF.com**: Alta Oosthuizen (bl). **55 123RF.com**: Gleb Ivanov (tl). **Dorling Kindersley**: The National Birds of Prey Centre (cra). **57 123RF.com**: Vasin Leenanuruksa (bl). **58 123RF.com**: Vasiliy Vishnevskiy (cr)

Cover images: *Front*: **123RF.com**: Steve Byland (clb); **Dreamstime.com**: Brebca (crb), Mikelane45 (tc), Mustafanc (cla); **iStockphoto.com**: BMacKenziePhotography (tr);
Back: **Dorling Kindersley**: Barnabas Kindersley, Natural History Museum, London (crb)

All other images © Dorling Kindersley
For further information see: www.dkimages.com

A WORLD OF IDEAS:
SEE ALL THERE IS TO KNOW
www.dk.com

Contents

- 8 Looking at birds
- 10 What is a bird?
- 12 Feathered friends
- 14 Taking to the air
- 16 Patterns in the air
- 18 From soaring to bounding
- 20 Finding a mate
- 22 Eggs and hatching
- 24 The first days
- 26 The first flight
- 28 Good parents
- 30 Cup-shaped nests
- 32 Strange nests
- 34 Cleaning and preening
- 36 Feeding habits
- 38 Meat-eating birds
- 40 Night hunters
- 42 Bird territories
- 44 Flying away
- 46 Birds of the sea
- 48 Birds of the shore
- 50 Freshwater birds
- 52 Woodland birds
- 54 Desert and grassland birds
- 56 Tropical birds
- 58 City birds
- 60 Index
- 61 Acknowledgements

Looking at birds

You may not always notice birds, but they are all over the place – in the garden, by the seashore, in the city. If you become a birdwatcher, soon you will begin to learn all sorts of things about birds – how they feed, how they fly, and the different sounds that they make.

House sparrow
This cheeky bird is found in gardens and cities across the world. You can recognize the male by its brown back, grey crown, and black bib.

Grey crown

Black bib

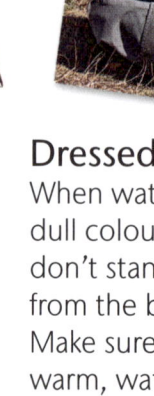

Dressed for the part
When watching birds, wear dull colours so that you don't stand out too much from the background. Make sure you have some warm, waterproof clothing in case it gets cold or wet.

No bird likes noise, so be as quiet as you can when watching birds!

> The best kind of notebook to use is a spiral-bound one with a stiff back. Jot down the shape of the bird you see, its colour, and the way it flies.

HOW TO DRAW A BIRD

The best way to remember a bird you see is to draw it. It is easier than you think to draw a bird. Build up your sketch from simple shapes.

1. Draw two circles — one for the head and one for the body.

2. Add the neck, beak, and legs.

3. Fill in the pattern of the feathers next.

1. Use half a circle for the body of a waterbird.

1. When drawing a bird in flight, start with two circles.

2. Add the wings, tail, neck, and beak. Is the head held out or tucked in?

3. Add in the wing details.

What is a bird?

Birds come in many shapes and sizes, but there are things that unite them. All birds are covered in feathers for warmth. They all have two wings, although not all birds can fly. All birds have beaks and lay eggs, and their legs and feet are covered in small scales.

Long, sharp beaks are good for finding food in soil or vegetation.

Birds have many feathers.

Spotting starlings
There are about 10,000 species of bird, and each one has its own special features. You can identify a starling by its shiny black feathers mixed with a purple or green sheen. In winter, its feathers are speckled white.

A bird's hollow, lightweight beak is made of horny material, and it is very strong.

Underneath its skin
Here is a starling without its skin! You have lots of bones under your skin, too. But a bird's bones contain many air spaces. These make the bones light for flying. A bird has very long legs – so what looks like its knees are really its ankles.

Ankle

The starling has a big keel, or breast bone. The powerful muscles that make wings beat are attached to this bone.

BIRD BEAKS

Birds have no hands, so they use their beaks to preen, build nests, and to pick up or tear up food. Different beaks are suited to eating different foods.

Many ducks feed by dabbling. They open and shut their beaks to take in water and strain out food.

Goshawks are meat-eaters. They have strong, hooked beaks for tearing apart flesh.

The greenfinch is a seed-eater, so its short, thick beak is strong enough to crack open hard seeds.

FANCY FOOTWORK

Birds may use their feet for perching in trees, running, or swimming. Some birds use their feet to catch prey.

Many birds that live in lakes and rivers have webbed feet for paddling.

The feet of birds of prey have long claws for gripping their prey.

Perching birds have one toe that points backwards to grasp branches.

Feathered friends

Birds are the only animals with feathers. A large bird, such as a swan, may have more than 25,000 feathers, and even a tiny hummingbird has almost 1,000. Feathers keep birds warm and dry and allow them to fly. A bird's feathers come in many beautiful colours and shapes.

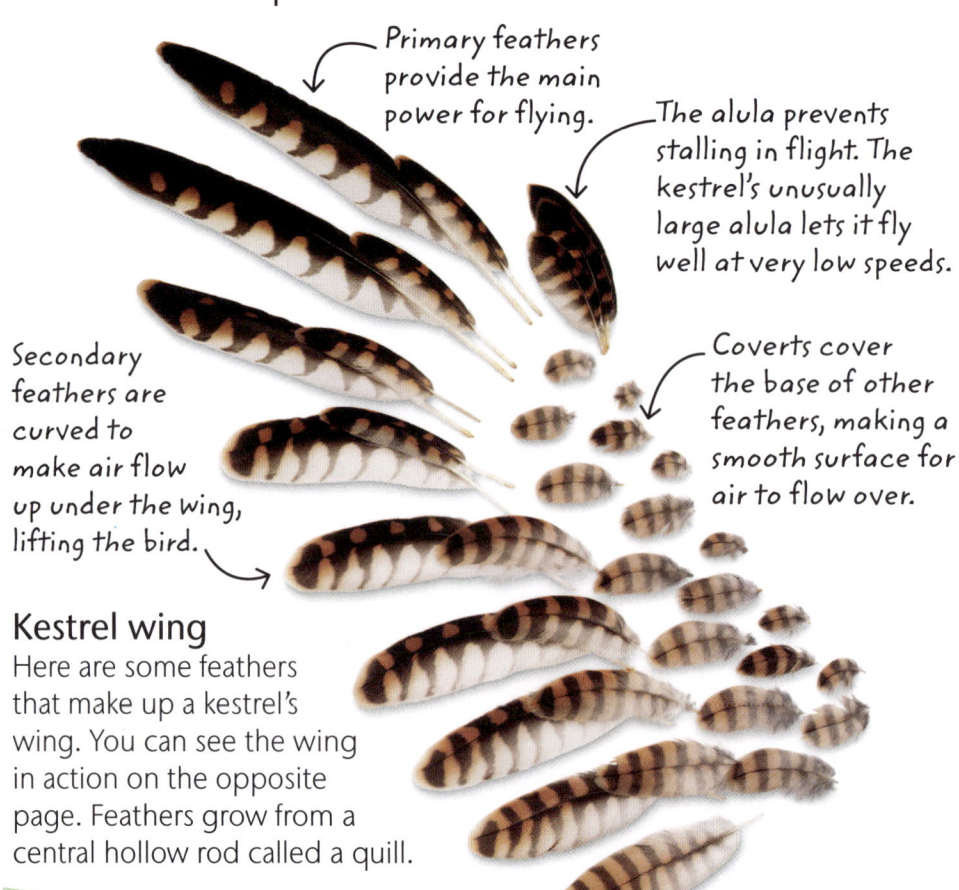

Primary feathers provide the main power for flying.

The alula prevents stalling in flight. The kestrel's unusually large alula lets it fly well at very low speeds.

Secondary feathers are curved to make air flow up under the wing, lifting the bird.

Coverts cover the base of other feathers, making a smooth surface for air to flow over.

Kestrel wing

Here are some feathers that make up a kestrel's wing. You can see the wing in action on the opposite page. Feathers grow from a central hollow rod called a quill.

Feather forms

A kestrel uses its long wing and tail feathers for flying. As it beats its wings down, the kestrel spreads its feathers out to press against the air. Like all birds, it has other feathers that are not used for flight. Smaller feathers cover the rest of the body, making it waterproof and windproof. Fluffy down feathers underneath keep the bird warm.

Hanging out to dry

A cormorant squeezes the air out of its feathers so it can dive and travel under water more easily, in search of fish. Afterwards, it spends a long time with its wings spread, drying them out.

Tail feathers act as a rudder for steering. They can also be lowered and spread out to act as a brake.

FINDING FEATHERS

Start collecting any feathers that you find in the garden, on the beach, or in the woods. Fix them to paper with sticky tape, or put them in clear plastic wallets. Make notes about where and when you found them, and label as many as possible.

Soft fringes on the edges of an owl's feathers muffle any noise made by the wings in flight, as it approaches a mouse.

The down at the base of a buzzard's coverts keeps it warm.

Taking to the air

A bird stays in the air by flapping its wings. As it pulls its wings down, the feathers push against the air, moving the bird up and forwards.

The feathers twist to let air through as the wings rise.

Fast fliers
Pigeons are powerful and speedy fliers. They are good at taking off in a hurry, and can fly for many hours without a break. Some pigeons are specially trained for racing. You can recognize racing pigeons because they often have rings around their legs, showing who they belong to.

With a few flaps, it is airborne.

The owl springs into the air with a kick of its feet.

Silent flight
Compared to the pigeon, the barn owl has broad wings and a slow, silent flight. It flaps its way over fields and hedges, watching and listening for small animals. Because it is so quiet, it can swoop onto prey without giving itself away.

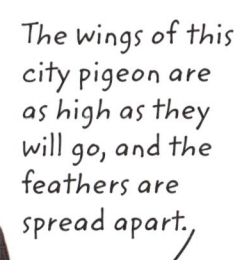

The wings of this city pigeon are as high as they will go, and the feathers are spread apart.

As the pigeon pulls its wings downwards, the feathers flatten out to make a single surface.

The feathers separate as the wings begin to rise again. They start to flick upwards, ready for the next beat of the wings.

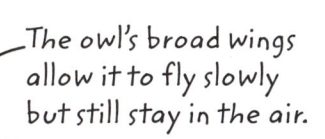

The owl's broad wings allow it to fly slowly but still stay in the air.

Happy landing

Landing safely is an important part of flying. The bird has to slow down at just the right time so that it drops gently to the ground. Young birds have to practise before they can land properly.

When the owl spots a mouse or vole, it starts to drop, using its wings as brakes, and swings its legs down.

Legs and feet are extended, ready to seize prey.

15

Patterns in the air

When you see a bird in flight, notice the pattern it makes. Different kinds of birds fly in different ways. Large heavy birds, such as ducks, flap their wings all the time. Many smaller birds save their energy by gliding between flaps. Some birds hover in the air as they search for prey or feed at flowers.

A fulmar's long, narrow wings help it to glide.

Gliding
The fulmar soars upwards on the rising air currents that form when the wind blowing from the sea meets the cliffs. Then it glides slowly down across the sea. It can travel a long way without flapping its wings at all.

Look for birds gliding near sea cliffs.

Hovering
The kestrel beats its wings forwards and spreads its tail feathers in order to hover. Doing this, it can spot small rodents, such as voles or mice, on the ground below. Look out for kestrels hovering over grass verges or patches of rough grassland.

Tail fanned out for balance

Large wings and powerful flight muscles lift the heavy body.

The mallard sticks its neck out when it flies.

If you spot a mallard flying over open ground, it is probably on its way to a lake or a river.

Straight line
Ducks, such as mallards, and geese often fly in V formation or in straight lines, beating their wings all the time.

DRAWING FLIGHT PATTERNS
Quick sketches of bird's flight can help to identify the bird, even if it is a long way off. Draw an outline of the shape the bird makes in flight, then indicate the way it flies with arrows.

From soaring to bounding

Meat-eating birds often need to fly long distances in search of a meal. To save energy, they soar (glide) on air currents. Many smaller birds do not need to fly so far. Some keep close to hedges and trees, where their enemies will not spot them.

Soaring
Eagles and vultures soar on thermals (warm bubbles of rising air), so they don't have to flap their wings much. In this way, they can keep an eye on the ground, and prey, and save energy as well!

Tail is fanned out.

Where do they soar?
Soaring birds go where the thermals are – over mountains, canyons, and wide open plains.

The California condor can glide for hours with its huge wings.

Hummingbirds hover in front of flowers as they sip the sweet nectar. The nectar in flowers gives the hummingbirds energy.

Flying backwards
Hummingbirds live in the Americas, and are the only birds that can fly sideways, forwards, and backwards. They are also the best hoverers of all. They need to hover to feed on nectar from flowers.

Stooping
The peregrine falcon swoops on other smaller birds in a vertical dive known as a stoop. Spot the sky-diver near cliffs or tall buildings in towns.

Bounding
Blue tits and many other small birds have a slightly bounding flight. They flap their wings in short bursts, then rest and glide. This saves energy.

Although this flight pattern is slightly exaggerated, small birds look as if they are bouncing up and down on the end of elastic!

Blue tits close their wings in between bursts of flapping.

Finding a mate

Before it can breed, a bird has to find a partner. Courtship is the way of attracting a mate that is of the right age and sex, and, most important, of the same type. Usually, the male attracts the female. If she is impressed by his courtship behaviour or his bright colours, she will mate with him and lay eggs.

Red balloon
Frigatebirds spend most of their lives flying high up over the sea. They nest on tropical islands. Each male bird picks a site for the nest, and then attracts a mate by blowing up his special pouch.

The male has a pouch of stretchy skin on the front of his throat. When the female comes near, he blows up his pouch, rattles his beak against it, and flaps his wings.

A frigatebird's wings are wide than the height of a man.

Hanging about

The male blue bird-of-paradise attracts a mate by opening his wings, and tipping forward until he is hanging upside-down, by his feet. This bird lives in tropical rainforests in New Guinea. Many other species in its family also have spectacular courtship displays.

When the male hangs upside-down, his dazzling blue feathers open up like a fan.

Friend or foe?

These Arctic terns look as though they are fighting over a fish. But they are courting. The male offers his partner the fish as a gift. The two birds then fly off together calling.

Bird bonding

Once the terns have landed, the female must accept the fish from the male one last time. This shows that she is willing to pair up. Many male birds give their partners food when they are courting. This helps to make a bond between the pair.

Eggs and hatching

A bird's egg is a living package protected by a hard shell. When it is newly laid, the egg contains just the yolk and the clear part. The parent keeps the egg warm by sitting on it, or "incubating" it. The yolk nourishes the growing bird, and after a few weeks it is ready to hatch.

One of a kind
Many guillemot eggs have spots or streaks. Parents can recognize their own egg by its unique pattern.

Jungle giant
The cassowary is a huge flightless bird from tropical forests in New Guinea and Australia. The female lays up to six enormous eggs.

Blue egg
The American robin lays about four blue eggs.

Ground nester
The curlew nests on the ground. Its speckled eggs are well camouflaged.

Tiny eggs
A hummingbird's nest has enough room for two pea-sized eggs.

Remember — never touch birds' eggs in the wild.

Into the outside world

If you tap an egg with a spoon, its shell will quickly break. However, imagine how hard the same job is for a baby bird. It has to break the shell from the inside. It has a special egg-tooth on the top of its bill, so it can chip through the shell. Here you can see how a duckling breaks out.

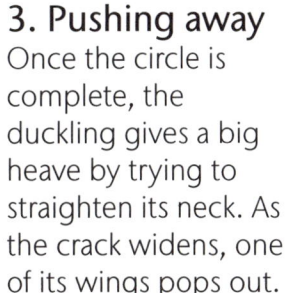

1. Making a hole
The duckling's hardest task comes first. Using its beak, it chips away at the blunt end of the egg until it has made a hole. Then it rests.

2. Round and round
Next, the duckling hammers away at the shell. It turns all the time, so that it cuts in a circle.

3. Pushing away
Once the circle is complete, the duckling gives a big heave by trying to straighten its neck. As the crack widens, one of its wings pops out.

4. Off with the top
Suddenly, the blunt end of the egg comes away as the duckling gives a final push.

5. Breaking out
The duckling falls out of the egg. Its wet feathers cling together, making it look bedraggled.

6. Drying off
Within two or three hours, the duckling's feathers have dried out and turned fluffy. It cannot fly yet, but it can run around and is ready for its first swim.

The first days

A duckling can feed itself when it is just a day old. But not all birds are like this. Many are blind and helpless when they hatch, and they rely on their parents to bring food to them. For adult blue tits, this means many days of hard work.

Eyes are not yet fully formed.

Feathers on wings

Feathers grow in a line along the back.

1. The new family
These baby blue tits are just four days old. They are blind and bald, and hardly look like birds at all. When one of their parents arrives at the nest with food, they open their beaks wide and stretch upwards.

2. Growing feathers
By the time the young birds are six days old, their feathers have started to grow.

Many baby birds have special coloured patterns inside their mouths. These show the parents where to put the food.

By the time they are ready to fly, many young birds are heavier than their parents. They are so big that they can hardly fit in the nest.

Eyes are fully open.

Wing feathers are protected by waxy tubes.

Eyes are beginning to open.

Tips of wing feathers are beginning to appear.

3. Fast food
The baby birds are now nine days old. Their parents bring them food almost once a minute, and so the nestlings quickly put on weight.

4. Growing up
Thirteen days after hatching, the nestlings are starting to look like their parents. Within a week, their wing and tail feathers will be fully grown, and they will be ready to fly.

The first flight

Baby birds know how to fly naturally, so they do not have to learn to fly. However, they do need to practise in order to learn how to twist and turn in the air, and how to land without falling on their faces.

A baby chaffinch makes its first flight, as its parents call out to encourage it.

Its flight feathers are not fully grown.

Follow the leader

At first, baby chaffinches stay safely hidden among the branches near their nest. After a few days, they can fly quite well. Then the young birds follow their parents around as they hunt for food. This saves the parents time and energy, as they no longer have to carry food back to the nest.

Brave babies
Little auks nest in the Arctic on cliff ledges high above the sea, where most of their enemies cannot reach them. On their very first flight, the baby auks must reach the sea below. There they will learn how to catch fish to eat. If they don't reach the sea, they will crash-land on the rocks.

Look out below!
The mandarin duck lays her eggs in a tree hole high above the ground, out of reach of foxes and other enemies. Before the ducklings are a day old, they must leap out of the tree. Their mother waits on the ground below, calling to them to follow her. When they have all landed safely, she will lead them to water and food.

Before landing, the baby chaffinch lowers its wing and tail to slow down. It then lowers its legs to absorb the shock as it hits the ground.

Mandarin ducklings spread their tiny wings and feet to slow their fall. Amazingly, they manage to land without getting hurt.

Good parents

Most new parents have to work very hard when a baby arrives, and birds are no exception. Newborn birds are usually helpless, so their parents have to feed them, keep them clean, and guard them against other animals that may want to eat them. Most parent birds tuck the chicks under their feathers to keep them warm or to shade them from the hot Sun.

Egg imposter
European cuckoo parents avoid looking after their young by laying their eggs in other birds' nests. When the baby cuckoo hatches, it pushes the others out of the nest. This cuckoo is bigger than its foster parents, but they continue to feed it.

Penguin parents
Penguins come ashore to rear their chicks. However, they need to travel far out to sea to hunt for fish or other marine prey. The parents take turns looking after the chick. One parent stays with the chick while the other goes out to sea to fish.

Penguin parents look after their chicks until they grow a coat of stiff waterproof feathers.

The penguin chick has a thick fluffy coat, but it still huddles against its parent to keep warm.

Light as a feather

Swans lay their eggs in big nests on river banks. Baby swans can swim and find their own food soon after they hatch. They are so light that they float easily on water. Every day their parents lead them to safe places to feed. Swans can be very fierce when they are guarding their young. They will attack any animal that comes too close, even humans – so be careful if you see them.

Baby swans are called cygnets. These cygnets are enjoying a ride on their father's back, safe and warm among his feathers.

Reaching for a fish

A pelican chick reaches far inside its parent's beak in search of food. The parent pelican flies along the coast or over lakes and catches lots of fish. It swallows them all and flies home. Then it brings the fish back up for the chick to eat.

Parent peckers

A hungry herring gull chick pecks at the bright red spot at the tip of its parent's beak. This persuades its parent to bring up food for the chick to eat.

Herring gull chicks are not as brightly coloured as their parents. This helps them hide from foxes, bigger gulls, and other enemies.

Cup-shaped nests

A bird's nest is where it lays its eggs and raises its young. The nest helps to keep the eggs and baby birds sheltered and warm. Many birds build cup-shaped nests high above the ground in trees.

Chaffinch nest

The chaffinch builds its nest in a small fork in a bush or tree. It is made of grass, moss, and roots, and lined with feathers and hair to keep the eggs warm.

Hard work

The female chaffinch has to make several hundred trips to collect all the right material in order to build a nest. She decorates the outside with lichen, which makes the nest hard to find.

By turning round slowly in the nest, and using its breast to push, the chaffinch makes the cup shape.

A hard bed
Instead of a downy bed, baby song thrushes have to sleep on a hard bed of mud. The song thrush makes a cup-shaped nest of roots, hairs, and grass, then finally adds a thin lining of wet mud.

When the mud dries, it becomes hard and strong.

Mud collector
The female song thrush collects grass, roots, dead leaves, twigs, and also wet mud from puddles.

Nest ingredients
Pieces of sheep's wool, spiders' webs, and even human hair and ribbons have all been found woven into birds' nests.

Pieces of tree bark give a nest strength.

Sheep's wool caught on barbed wire fences makes a warm nest lining.

Mud is picked up from puddles and stream banks.

Twigs and leaves

Strange nests

Not all nests are cup-shaped. Some birds just scrape hollows in the ground. Others use strange materials: tiny cave swiftlets make little cup-shaped nests of their own spit, which hardens as it dries on the cave wall. The mallee fowl builds a huge mound of sand and buries its eggs in the middle.

The chicks live in the round part of the nest.

Weaver bird nest
Weavers are birds that make their nests by weaving lots of pieces of grass together. Their nests are light and airy, but also strong and showerproof. The long "tunnel" leading to the nest stops snakes and other predators getting inside to eat the eggs and the young.

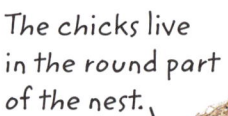

Weaving a home
The male weaver bird starts with a knotted ring hanging from a tree. Then it weaves fresh grass in and out until the nest is completed.

Entrance to nest

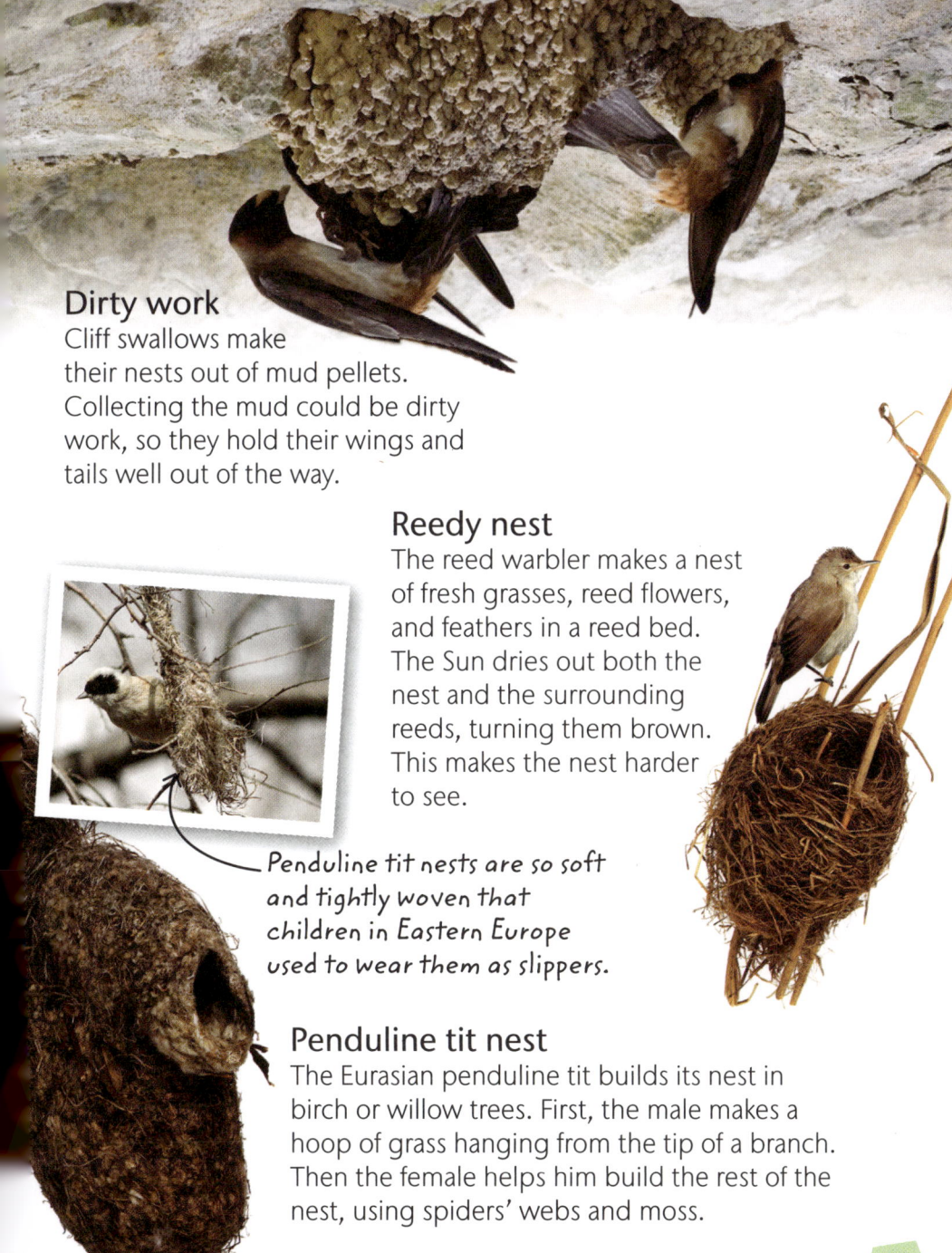

Dirty work
Cliff swallows make their nests out of mud pellets. Collecting the mud could be dirty work, so they hold their wings and tails well out of the way.

Reedy nest
The reed warbler makes a nest of fresh grasses, reed flowers, and feathers in a reed bed. The Sun dries out both the nest and the surrounding reeds, turning them brown. This makes the nest harder to see.

Penduline tit nests are so soft and tightly woven that children in Eastern Europe used to wear them as slippers.

Penduline tit nest
The Eurasian penduline tit builds its nest in birch or willow trees. First, the male makes a hoop of grass hanging from the tip of a branch. Then the female helps him build the rest of the nest, using spiders' webs and moss.

Cleaning and preening

Birds must keep their feathers in perfect condition. If they are dirty or ruffled, it is difficult to fly and keep warm, so they need constant care. A good place to watch birds clean their feathers is by a bird bath or a puddle in the park. Afterwards, they comb the feathers with their beaks. This is called preening.

The starling uses its beak to zip up the branches, or barbs, of its feathers.

Preening time
The starling runs each ruffled feather through its beak to make them smooth. Then it uses its beak to collect oil from a preen gland at the base of its tail. It wipes the oil over its feathers to condition or waterproof them.

Unzipped, ruffled feather

Zipped up feather

Zipped up
The little branches of each feather have tiny hooks that can be zipped up to make a smooth strong surface for flying.

Splish splash
A good splash in the water is the first step in a bird's cleaning routine. Bathing birds fluff up their feathers, then duck down and use their wings to splash water over their bodies.

A corn bunting keeps an eye out for danger while it washes its feathers.

MAKE A BIRD BATH
You can make a bird bath from a dustbin lid, or a plant-pot saucer, and some bricks. Birds need a gentle slope so they can paddle in and out, and a rough surface so they don't slip.

1. Set three bricks in a triangle on flat ground in the open. Put the lid upside-down on the bricks. Add a layer of clean small stones and a few larger pebbles. Fill with water.

2. Keep the bath full and make sure the water does not freeze in winter. Rinse it out every so often to keep the water clean.

3. It's important that you place the bird bath far away from trees, bushes, or other places that a cat could hide, so it cannot pounce on birds while they are drinking or bathing.

Feeding habits

Birds have many different ways of feeding. Swifts catch insects on the wing. Starlings push their beaks into the soil to seize grubs. Herons use their bills for spearing fish, while finches use their beaks for cracking seeds.

Snail smasher
If you find broken snail shells in your garden, you may have discovered a song thrush's anvil. The thrush smashes open shells on a favourite stone to get the snail inside.

Floating umbrella
When the black heron hunts fish, it lowers its head and neck and spreads its wings around until they meet in front. This shades the water from the Sun, making it easier to spot fish.

Acrobatic birds
Tits are the acrobats of the bird world. They are often seen hanging upside down from bird feeders, or from twigs as they search for insects.

FEED THE BIRDS

A feeding bell on a rope attracts chickadees and other tits, and provides a safe feeding place out of reach of cats. To make a feeding bell, you'll need a yoghurt pot, a piece of strong string, some bird food (seeds, nuts, raisins, crumbs), some melted fat (lard, suet, or dripping) and a mixing bowl.

1. Ask an adult to help you make a small hole in the bottom of the pot. Thread the string through and secure it with a large knot or tie a small twig on the end.

2. ASK AN ADULT to warm the fat until it melts. Then mix in the bird food in a bowl.

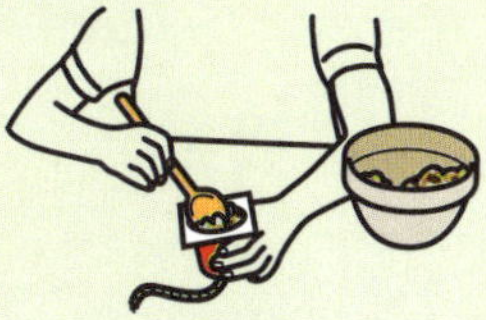

3. Spoon the mixture into the pot and leave it in a cool place until it hardens.

4. Hang the bell on a tree in the garden or on the side of a bird table. Watch for tits performing as they feed.

Meal in a nutshell

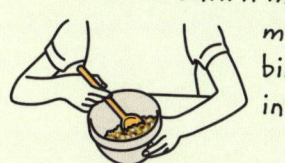

The nuthatch wedges an acorn or hazelnut into a crack in tree bark, then hammers it open to reach the seed inside. If you find a nut shell with a jagged hole or split in two, it will have been eaten by a bird.

Crossed bill

Crossbills have a unique bill which crosses over at the tips. It is designed to prize seeds out of spruce or pine cones, but it can also pick bark off tree trunks to reach insects.

Meat-eating birds

There are many meat-eaters in the bird world. The ones that hunt by swooping and attacking with their claws are called birds of prey. Most birds of prey watch out for food from high in the air, so this is the best place to look for them.

Fishing from the air
The majestic bald eagle fishes from the air. It flaps over the water, snatches up a fish in its claws, then flies away with it to a perch. Bald eagles are usually seen near lakes, rivers, and coasts.

The bald eagle uses its huge, hooked beak to pull apart fish and other animals that it catches.

Feathered hunters
Many other birds, such as shrikes, use their beak rather than their claws to catch small animals and insects. Shrikes store their food by spearing it on long thorns.

Eyes in the sky
Vultures soar high in the sky in search of food. They also keep close watch on each other. When one bird spots a meal, others quickly follow it.

Pinpointing prey
The kestrel is one of the few birds of prey that can hover. It hangs in the air as it pinpoints its prey, then drops down to catch it in its claws.

Most vultures have no feathers on their heads, as blood would make their feathers dirty when they feed. The king vulture is unusual because its head is brightly coloured.

Cleaning up
Vultures may not be very popular birds, but they do a very useful job by eating up the remains of dead animals. They peck holes in the carcasses, and stretch out their long necks to feed inside.

Night hunters

When the Sun sets, most birds settle down for the night. Owls are different. Most of them spend the day asleep, and wake up when it gets dark. Owls hunt small animals at night, using their sensitive eyes and ears.

These feathery tufts look like ears, but the real ears are lower down, hidden at the sides of the owl's face.

Owls have "binocular" vision. This means that both their eyes point in the same direction, just like ours. This way of seeing lets an owl know exactly how far away its prey is.

Still life

The long-eared owl spends the day perched motionless on a branch. It is very difficult to see, because its feathers make it look just like a piece of wood. This owl has long "ear" tufts that it can raise or lower. These help it to recognize other owls of the same type, or species.

The barn owl

The barn owl lives all over the world, from America to Australia. Like other owls, it has a bowl-shaped face. This guides sounds into its ears, which are hidden under its feathers.

The barn owl catches small animals with its claws, then carries them off in its beak. It swallows them whole.

Owls can see their prey by moonlight, or even by starlight.

WHAT'S ON THE MENU?

After an owl has eaten, it coughs up a pellet. This contains the bones and fur of its prey. Old pellets are quite safe to handle, and you can gently pull them apart with tweezers to see what an owl has been eating. The best place to look for pellets is in old barns, or around tree trunks.

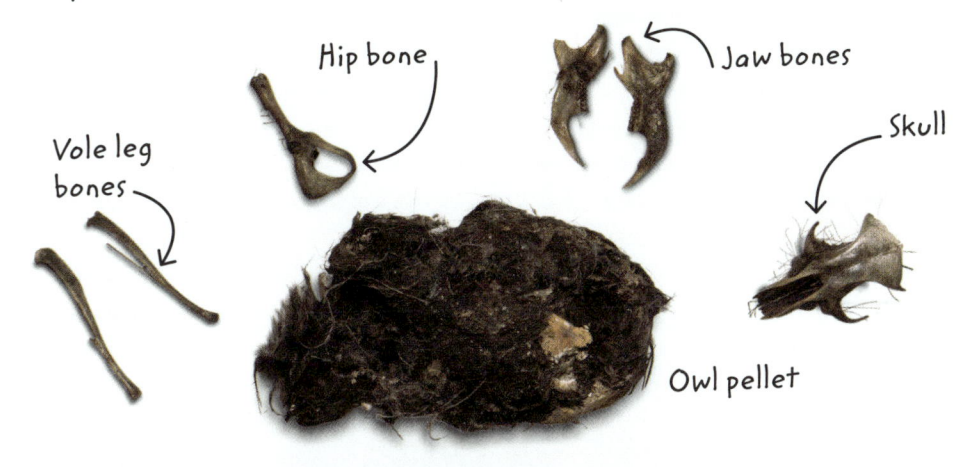

Vole leg bones

Hip bone

Jaw bones

Skull

Owl pellet

Bird territories

The world of birds is full of private property – pieces of land called territories. They are an important part of the way many birds live. By claiming a territory, a bird can make sure that it has somewhere to attract a mate, a place to nest, and enough space for a growing family.

Bird song
To us, bird song is just a pretty sound. However, to birds, it is a way of sending messages about their territories.

Eastern bluebirds sing from high perches so that they can be heard a long way off.

It's my garden!
Male European robins often set up territories in gardens. The owner sings loudly to tell other robins where his territory is. If another male robin flies into the territory, a battle quickly follows.

LISTEN AND LEARN
Most types of bird have a distinctive song or call. You will often hear a bird before you see it. Try recording birds singing on a smartphone or tablet. In some countries, you can download an app that will help you identify a bird from its song.

The female will mate with the male who puts on the best performance.

Forest showground
Male Andean cock-of-the-rocks gather in an arena of trees to display for watching females. They show off their feathers and squawk loudly.

Each male sits on a different branch, which is his territory. The displaying male bows and flaps its wings.

Keep your distance
Gannets are large seabirds that nest together on rocky cliffs and islands. Around each nest is a small territory, reaching just as far as the bird on the nest can stretch.

Pairs of nesting gannets have to stay beyond the "pecking distance" of their neighbours.

Flying away

Have you noticed how some birds disappear in winter? Have you ever wondered where they go? Many spend their lives in two different places. They spend winter where it is warmer. Then in spring, they fly away to raise their families where there is plenty of food. These journeys are migrations.

Flight of the snow goose

The snow goose breeds in the Arctic tundra, and migrates south to the Gulf of Mexico. Its journey is about 3,200 km (2,000 miles) long. The world's greatest bird traveller, the Arctic tern, on average makes a two-way trip of 70,000 km (43,500 miles) between the Arctic and Antarctic every year.

Wild geese migrate in V-shaped flocks. Flying in this formation uses less energy. Each bird gets a lift from the force of the bird in front.

COUNTING THE BIRDS

Here is a quick way to count the birds in a migrating flock. Make a circle with your thumb and first finger. Hold your arm out, and count the birds in the circle. Then see roughly how many circles it takes to cover the whole flock. Multiply the first number by the second to get the answer.

Herald of summer

According to an old English saying, "one swallow doesn't make a summer". But when barn swallows arrive, you can be sure that summer is not far behind. In autumn, young swallows migrate with their parents. The following spring, many find their way from southern Africa back to Europe by instinct.

Travelling geese

Barnacle geese travel in flocks that can contain thousands of birds. They pause on their long journey to rest and feed at their favourite lakes. At night, you can hear the geese calling as they fly overhead. They use the Sun and stars as a compass to help them find their way.

Birds of the sea

Many seabirds make their homes on rocky cliffs, where they are safer from their enemies. Each bird has its favourite nesting place. The puffin likes grassy slopes at the top of cliffs, while gannets are quite happy on bare rock. Seabirds often spend the winter months far out at sea and come ashore to breed.

Diving gannets
Gannets feed on fish such as mackerel and herring. A gannet has a special shock-absorbing layer under its skin. This protects it when it dives into the water.

Gannets always breed together, in groups of up to 50,000 nests.

Gannets dive head-first into the sea to catch fish. They fold their wings back before they hit the water.

Clifftop clowns

With their large, striped beaks and bright orange feet, puffins are hard to miss. They tunnel in soft ground on grassy slopes and islands, and catch fish out at sea.

Short wings

Puffins can hold lots of fish at once in their beaks.

Webbed feet spread out for landing

Puffins use old rabbit burrows as nests or dig burrows for themselves using their beaks.

Perched on the edge

The guillemot (gill-i-mot) makes no nest at all, but lays its single egg on a cliff ledge. The parent bird holds the egg in its feet. Guillemots nest in big, noisy colonies.

The guillemot's egg is pear-shaped, so that it rolls around in a circle instead of falling off the cliff.

Birds of the shore

Sandy beaches are fine for swimming and sun-bathing, but if you want to watch shore birds, the thing to look for is lots of sticky mud. Muddy shores contain a hidden world of small animals, from worms to tiny snails, and many different kinds of birds feed on them. Most of these birds are waders, which means they have long legs and probing beaks.

Beak with a bend
You don't have to be the world's cleverest birdwatcher to recognize an avocet, because it is one of the few birds with a beak that curves upwards.

The Eurasian avocet moves its beak from side to side in the water, snapping it shut when it feels food.

Although it can swim, the avocet usually strides through the water on its long legs. Its legs are so long that they trail behind the avocet when it flies.

A feast in the mud
The bar-tailed godwit reaches deep into the mud with its long beak, which snaps open and shut just like a pair of tweezers.

The stone turner

Flocks of turnstones can be seen walking along the shore in search of food. These small birds turn over stones with their probing beaks, hoping to find crabs and other small animals.

Shell-smasher

If you have ever collected seashells, you will know how tough they are. However, small shells are no match for the oystercatcher. With sharp blows of its strong, rod-like beak, it smashes them open and eats the soft animal inside.

Strong, orange beak

Anything goes

Some birds are very choosy about what they eat, but the herring gull will feed on almost anything. Dead fish, baby birds, earthworms, and rotting rubbish are all on the menu when it looks for food.

The herring gull uses its powerful beak to pull apart its food, and also to peck its way to the front in the scramble to eat.

Freshwater birds

Ponds, streams, rivers, and lakes are often teeming with small animals and plants. Tiny fish, young insects, shrimps, and waterweed are all food for freshwater birds. Most of these birds feed by swimming on the surface or diving, while others wade through the shallows. However, kingfishers catch small fish by diving at them from a perch.

Ducks and drakes
Mallards live on ponds, lakes, and streams. The male is called the "drake" and has a shiny green head. The female is called the "duck" and is drab and brown.

Tail in the air
Mallards feed in two ways. They either "up end" to reach food just below the surface, or they scoop small animals and plants off the surface.

Attack from the air

A good place to see a kingfisher is from a bridge. Here you can watch it darting up and down a stream or a river. A kingfisher spells danger to small fish. Once it catches a fish, it bashes its prey against a perch to stun it, then swallows the whole fish head-first.

You can recognize a Eurasian kingfisher by its bright turquoise feathers.

Kingfishers make nests in riverbank burrows. They peck away at the earth, then kick out the pieces.

The kingfisher plunges in head-first to catch a fish in its beak.

The roseate spoonbill's special diet makes its feathers pink.

A beak with two spoons

It is easy to see how spoonbills got their name. The ends of their beaks are broad and round, just like a pair of spoons. A spoonbill wades slowly through the water with its beak half-open and waves it from side-to-side. When it feels food, its two "spoons" close around it.

Woodland birds

Hundreds of different birds live in woods, and trees make safe homes for them. They build their nests high up among the leaves, or hidden inside hollow trunks. A good place to wait for birds is near a clearing, where you can spot them feeding on insects and seeds.

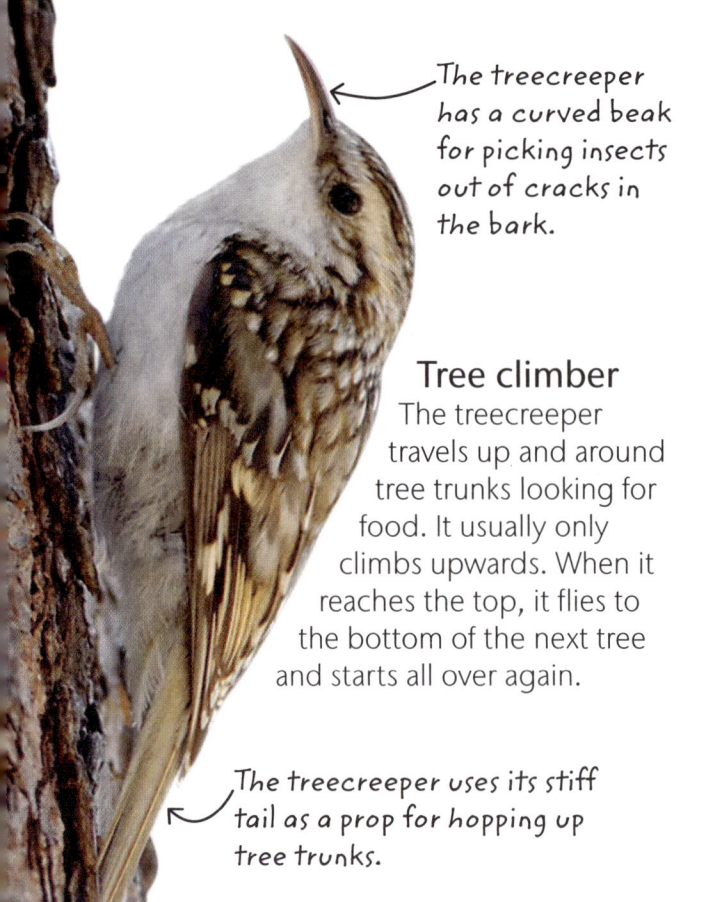

The treecreeper has a curved beak for picking insects out of cracks in the bark.

Tree climber
The treecreeper travels up and around tree trunks looking for food. It usually only climbs upwards. When it reaches the top, it flies to the bottom of the next tree and starts all over again.

Acorns away
The acorn woodpecker wedges acorns firmly into the bark of a favourite tree to make a winter food-store.

The treecreeper uses its stiff tail as a prop for hopping up tree trunks.

Woodpecker warning
You might hear this woodpecker before you see it! With its powerful beak, it drums loudly on dead wood to proclaim its territory. Woodpeckers also use their beaks to make nest holes in trees, and to drill into rotten tree trunks in search of grubs to eat.

The hairy woodpecker sits on its tail when it feeds its young.

Hidden in the leaves
The nightjar comes out at night to feed on moths. By day, it sits perfectly still on the rough ground. Its feathers match the dead leaves so well that it is almost impossible to spot the bird.

Forgotten trees
In autumn, look for jays collecting acorns. They bury them in the ground to eat later. However, the birds forget many of the hiding places, and in spring the acorns sprout into little oak trees.

Desert and grassland birds

Many hot desert and grassland birds seek shelter from the Sun's heat during the hottest part of the day, and a few only appear at night. However, in the daytime, watch for large birds high in the sky, and for flocks of small birds flitting around in search of seeds and insects. At sunrise and sunset, look out for desert birds at water holes.

Full speed ahead
America's roadrunner literally runs across the desert chasing lizards and snakes. It can reach speeds of 20 kph (12 mph). When in danger, it prefers to run rather than fly.

Thirsty chicks
Sandgrouse often fly as far as 30 km (19 miles) across the desert to find water. They have special breast feathers that soak up large amounts of water. The male sandgrouse soaks his feathers in a pool or water hole, then flies home. The thirsty chicks suck the water from his feathers.

The ostrich is the world's fastest two-legged runner. It can run at speeds of up to 70 kph (44 mph).

Female ostriches are brown.

Snake stalker
The secretary bird builds a nest of twigs and dead branches on the top of a thorn tree. This long-legged bird of prey stalks the grassland in search of snakes to eat, then bites off their heads before taking them home to feed to its chicks.

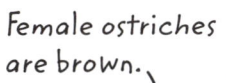

Big bird
Ostriches wander across dry African grasslands in search of food and water. They are the largest birds in the world. Some stand over 2.5m (8 ft) tall.

Ostriches are too big to fly, but their long legs carry them away from danger.

Tropical birds

You will see some of the most colourful birds in the world's tropical forests. Parrots and toucans live in the treetops, and male birds-of-paradise display their beautiful feathers to attract mates. Jungle fowl and pheasants roam the forest floor and hummingbirds hover at flowers, while eagles soar high overhead.

On the look-out
This sulphur-crested cockatoo is on guard duty. "Guards" stay up in the trees while the rest of the flock eats seeds on the ground. If there is any sign of danger, they will shriek a loud warning.

What toucans do
Toucans fly around the more open areas of tropical forests, calling out to each other with loud frog-like croaks. They nest in small tree holes and may use the same site the following year.

The toucan uses its huge beak to reach fruit hanging from branches.

Brilliant colours

There are lots of parrots in tropical forests. They use their strong hooked beaks to crack open nuts. Their beaks can also be a useful aid when climbing about in trees. Parrots usually fly around in small groups. Listen for their harsh cries, and look for their brilliant colours as they fly overhead.

A long tail helps this crimson rosella from Australia to balance as it twists and turns between the trees.

You can recognize the male jungle fowl by the large red "comb" on his head.

Tropical chickens

Asia's red jungle fowl is the domestic chicken's wild ancestor. Like chickens, jungle fowl live on the ground, where they scrape around for seeds.

The female jungle fowl has dull colours to hide her while she sits on her eggs on the forest floor.

City birds

Many birds – starlings, sparrows, pigeons, and even gulls – have learned to live with people. Small birds such as robins, tits, finches, and thrushes nest in hidden corners of city gardens, and peregrine falcons raise their young on tall buildings. In winter, watch for unusual visitors moving in from the country to feed on berries, rotting apples, and bird-table food.

Messy birds
City pigeons roost and nest on the ledges of buildings. Their droppings mess up city streets and statues, and are expensive to clean up.

Summer visitors
House martins build their mud nests under the eaves of city roofs. You can often spot their little white faces peering out. House martins are summer visitors to Europe, arriving in late April. After they have reared their young, they return to Africa in late September.

The house martin makes its nest out of mud. Sticky wet mud helps to glue the nest into position.

NEST BOXES

Many birds that nest in holes in trees in the wild will happily use wooden nest boxes in city gardens instead. You can help garden birds by putting up your own nest boxes on suitable trees or posts. They need to have a small opening just large enough for the birds to squeeze inside.

City scavengers

Magpies feed on almost anything, including scraps of food dropped on the street, and the eggs and young of smaller birds. Pigeons and thrushes often attack magpies to keep them away from their nests.

Look for the white crescent on a magpie's back as it flies.

Index

AB
auk, little 27
avocet, Eurasian 48

bathing 35
beaks 10, 11, 48
bird baths 35
bird-of-paradise 21, 56
birds of prey 11, 38, 39
birdwatching 8–9
bluebird, eastern 42
bonding 21
bones 10, 41
bounding flight 19
bunting, corn 35
buzzard 13

C
calls 42
cassowary 22
chaffinch 26, 27, 30
chicks 28, 29, 32
city birds 58–59
claws 11, 38
cleaning feathers 34–35
cock-of-the-rocks, Andean 43
cockatoo, sulphur-crested 56
condor, California 18
cormorant 13
courtship 20–21, 43
crossbill 37
cuckoo, European 28
cup-shaped nests 30–31
curlew 22

DE
desert birds 54–55
displays 20–21, 43
diving 46, 50
drawing birds 9
duck 11, 16–17, 23, 24, 27, 50

eagles 18, 38, 56
eggs 22–23, 47
eyes, owls 40

F
feathers 10, 12–13, 24–25, 34–35
feeding 36–41
feeding bell 37
feet 11
finches 36, 58
first days 24–25
flocks 44–45
flying 13, 18–19
freshwater birds 50–51
frigatebird 20
fulmar 16

G
gannet 43, 46
geese 17, 44, 45
gliding 16, 18
godwit, bar-tailed 48
goshawk 11
grassland birds 54–55
greenfinch 11
guillemot 22, 47
gulls 29, 49, 58

HJ
hatching 23
herons 36
hovering 17
hummingbird 12, 19, 22, 56
hunting 38–41

jay 53
jungle fowl 56, 57

KL
kestrel 12–13, 17, 39
kingfisher 50, 51

learning to fly, chicks 26–27
looking after, chicks 28–29

M
magpie 59
mallard 17, 50
mallee fowl 32
mandarin duck 27
martin, house 58
meat-eating birds 18, 38–39
migration 44–45

N O

nest boxes 59
nestlings 25, 28, 30–31
nests 30–33, 46–47
night hunters 40–41
nightjar 53
nuthatch 37

ostrich 55
owls 13, 14–15, 40, 41
oystercatcher 49

P R

parrots 56, 57
patterns in the air, flying 16–17
pelicans 29
pellets, owls 41
penguins 28
peregrine falcon 19, 58
pheasants 56
pigeons 14–15, 58, 59
preening feathers 34–35
puffin 46, 47

roadrunner 54
robins 22, 42
rosella, crimson 57

S

sandgrouse 54
seabirds 46–47
secretary bird 55
shore birds 48–49
shrikes 38
soaring 18

songs 42
sparrows 8, 58
spoonbill, roseate 51
starlings 10, 34, 36, 58
stooping 19
swallows 33, 45
swans 12, 29
swiftlet, cave 32
swifts 36

T

taking to the air, flying 14–15
tern, Arctic 21, 44
territories 42–43
thrushes 31, 36, 58, 59
tits 19, 24–25, 33, 36, 58
toucan 56
treecreeper 52
tropical birds 56–57
turnstone 49

V W

vultures 18, 39

waders 48–49
warbler, reed 33
water birds 50–51
weaver birds 32
wings 12–19
woodland birds 52–53
woodpeckers 52, 53

Acknowledgements

Dorling Kindersley would like to thank:

Simon Battensby for photography on pages 10 and 12.
Sharon Grant and Faith Nelson for design assistance.
Gin von Noorden and Kate Rasworth for editorial assistance and research.
Hilary Bird for the index.
Kim Taylor for special photography on pages 14–15, 23, 24–25, 26–27, 52.

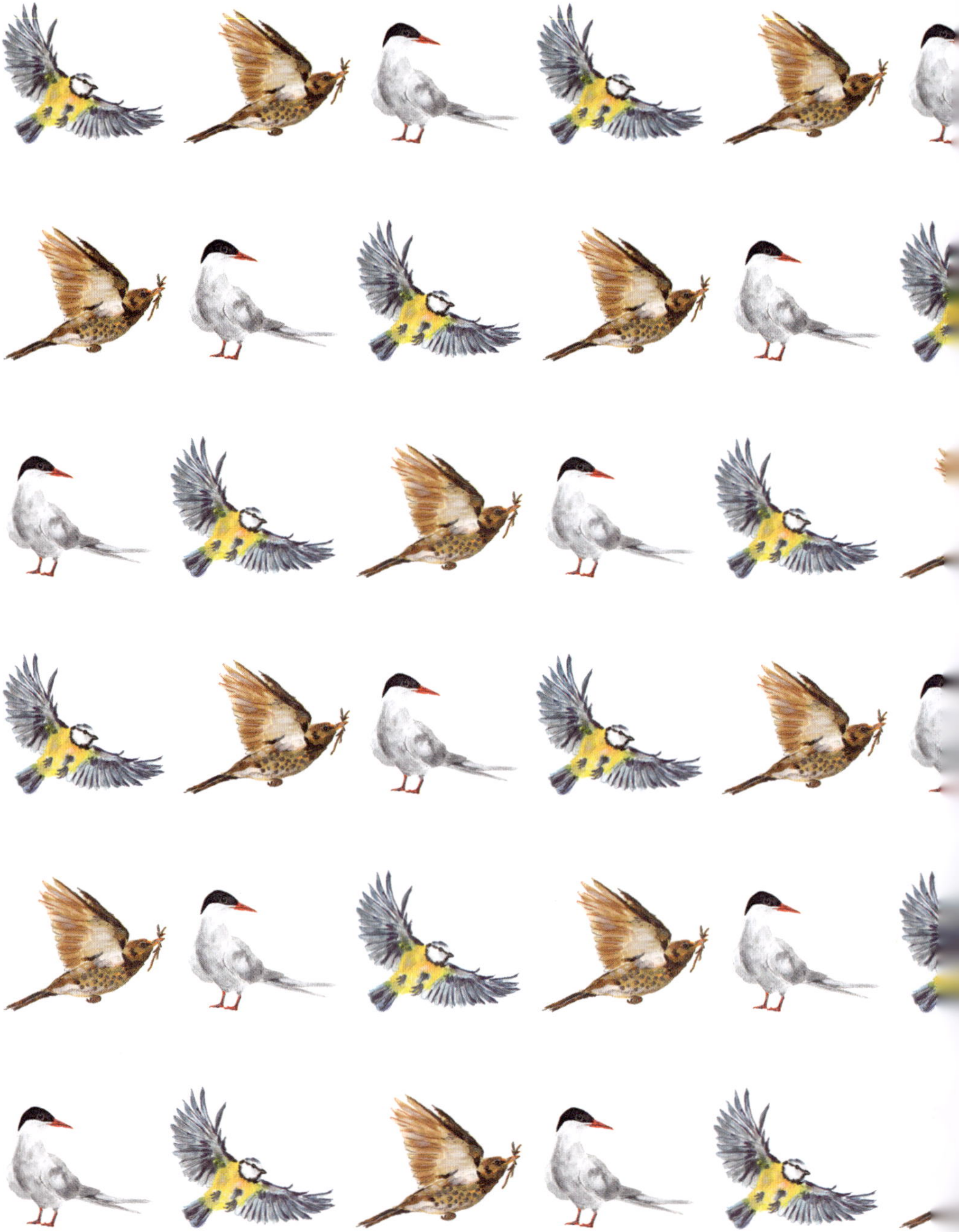

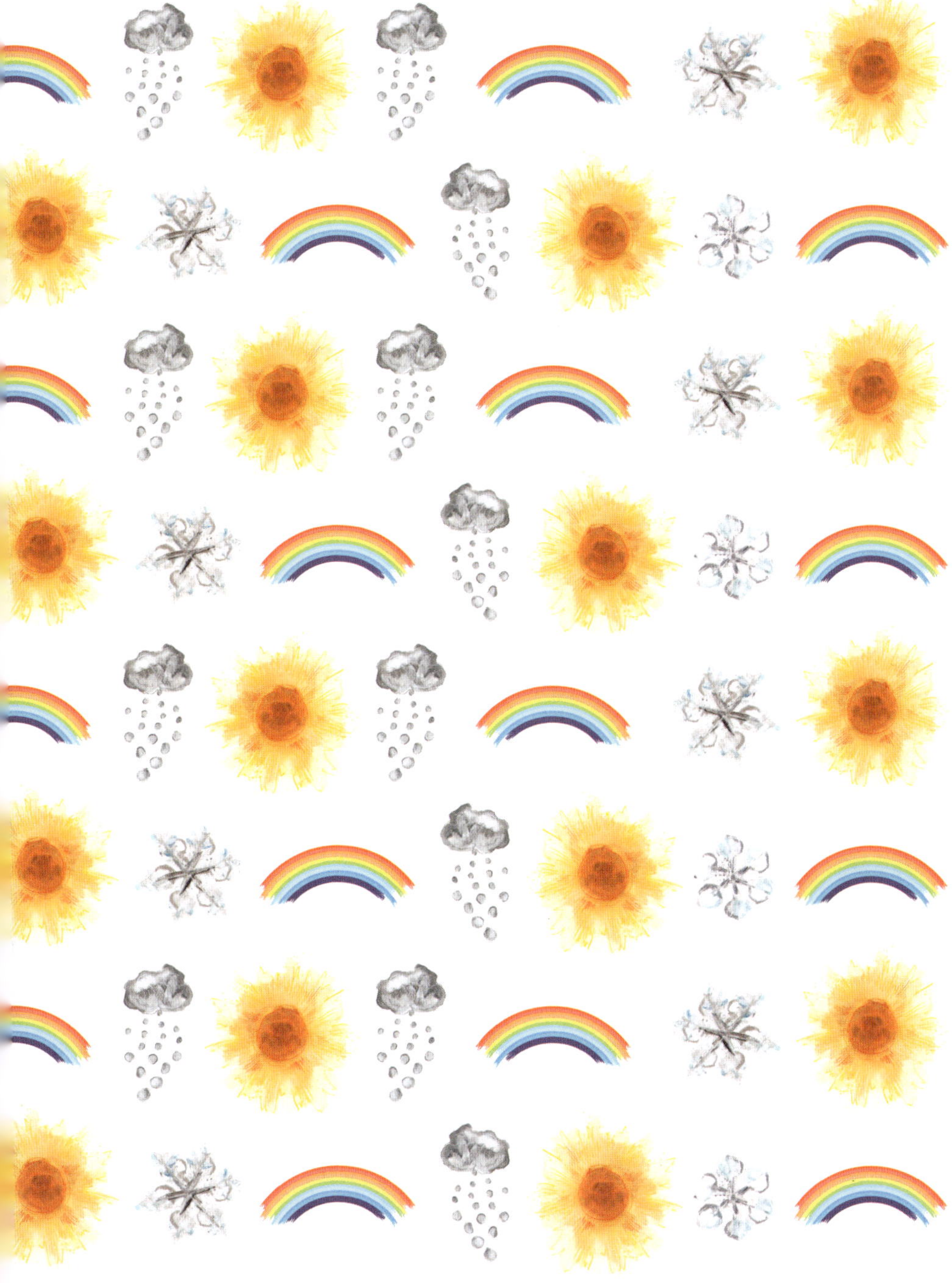

On cold nights, plants may get so cold that moisture in the air freezes onto them instantly, instead of forming liquid dew. This is called hoar frost.

Lightning flashes between the bottom of the thundercloud and the ground.

Sun

Igloos are dome-shaped houses built of solid blocks of snow.

"Wet" snow makes good snowballs.

Weather

Written by John Farndon
Consultant: John Woodward

DK

Penguin Random House

Senior editor Gill Pitts
Editor Olivia Stanford
Assistant editor Kritika Gupta
Editorial assistance Cécile Landau
Senior art editor Ann Cannings
Project art editor Yamini Panwar
Illustrators Abby Cook, Dan Crisp, Shahid Mahmood
Jacket co-ordinator Francesca Young
Jacket designers Dheeraj Arora, Amy Keast, Faith Nelson
DTP designers Dheeraj Singh, Jagtar Singh

Picture researcher Aditya Katyal
Producer, pre-production Nadine King
Producer Isabell Schart
Managing editors Soma B. Chowdhury, Laura Gilbert, Monica Saigal
Managing art editors Neha Ahuja Chowdhry, Diane Peyton Jones
Art director Martin Wilson
Publisher Sarah Larter
Publishing director Sophie Mitchell

Original edition
Project editor Christine Webb
Art editors Thomas Keenes, Carol Orbel
Senior editor Susan McKeever
Senior art editor Jacquie Gulliver
Production Catherine Semark
Editorial consultant Ron Lobeck
Illustrators John Bendall-Brunello, Julia Cobbold, Louis Mackay, Richard Ward

First published in Great Britain in 1992.
This edition first published in Great Britain in 2017 by
Dorling Kindersley Limited
80 Strand, London, WC2R 0RL

Copyright © 1992, 1997, 2017 Dorling Kindersley Limited
A Penguin Random House Company
8 7 6 5 4 3 2 1
001–308947–Nov/2017

All rights reserved.
No part of this publication may be reproduced, stored in or introduced into a retrieval system, or transmitted, in any form, or by any means (electronic, mechanical, photocopying, recording, or otherwise), without the prior written permission of the copyright owner.

A CIP catalogue record for this book is available from the British Library.
ISBN: 978-0-2412-8251-9

Printed and bound in China

The publisher would like to thank the following for their kind permission to reproduce their photographs:
(Key: a-above; b-below/bottom; c-centre; f-far; l-left; r-right; t-top)

4 123RF.com: Derrick Neill (tl); Taina Sohlman (cra). **Alamy Stock Photo:** Design Pics Inc (bl). **Dreamstime.com:** Dmytro Kozlov (b). **9 NASA:** (cr). **10 123RF.com:** Andrew Mayovskyy (crb). **Ann Cannings:** (cr). **Dreamstime.com:** Konart (bc). **11 123RF.com:** PaylessImages (cl). **Dreamstime.com:** Marsia16 (clb). **16 123RF.com:** andersonrise (cr); oasis15 (t, br). **18 Dreamstime.com:** Sabine Katzenberger (bl). **Rex by Shutterstock:** Amos Chapple (cr). **19 123RF.com:** (t). **20-21 123RF.com:** mrtwister (b). **22 123RF.com:** Thomas Fikar (b). **23 123RF.com:** Wasin Pummarin (t). **Getty Images:** Keystone (b). **24 123RF.com:** alexsol (cr); Taina Sohlman (bl). **Dreamstime.com:** Furtseff (tl). **25 123RF.com:** PaylessImages (t). **Alamy Stock Photo:** Andrew Rubtsov (crb). **26 Fotolia:** Alexandr Ozerov (cl). **27 Alamy Stock Photo:** Design Pics Inc (b). **Dreamstime.com:** Dmytro Kozlov (bl/Snowballs); Yael Weiss (cr). **29 123RF.com:** jezper (br). **30 iStockphoto.com:** Artur Synenko. **32 123RF.com:** Meghan Pusey Diaz / playalife2006 (b). **Corbis:** Warren Faidley (cr). **34 123RF.com:** Anton Yankovyi (cl). **34-35 Dreamstime.com:** Justin Hobson. **35 123RF.com:** Darko Komorski (cla); sebastien decoret (crb). **36 123RF.com:** smileus (br). **Alamy Stock Photo:** imageBROKER (cra). **39 Corbis:** Bettmann (c). **41 Dreamstime.com:** Nuralya (tr). **46-47 123RF.com:** Derrick Neill. **47 123RF.com:** Pornkamol Sirimongkolpanich (r). **48 Alamy Stock Photo:** United Archives GmbH (cl). **49 123RF.com:** manachai Phongruchiraphan (tl). **51 123RF.com:** Pablo Hidalgo (t). **Alamy Stock Photo:** Morley Read (b). **52 123RF.com:** Nikolai Grigoriev (t). **iStockphoto.com:** Heiko Küverling (bl). **54 123RF.com:** oceanfishing (cra). **PunchStock:** Design Pics (clb).

Cover images: Front: **Dreamstime.com:** Furtseff (tl), Motorolka (cr); **Getty Images:** DAJ (tc), MyLoupe (bl); Back: **Alamy Stock Photo:** Design Pics Inc (bl); **Dreamstime.com:** Gsk2013 (cl); **iStockphoto.com:** Artur Synenko (br); Spine: **Dreamstime.com:** Motorolka t/ (Maple Leaf)

All other images © Dorling Kindersley
For further information see: www.dkimages.com

**A WORLD OF IDEAS:
SEE ALL THERE IS TO KNOW**

www.dk.com

Contents

- 8 What is weather?
- 10 The seasons
- 12 The three clouds
- 14 Cloudspotting
- 16 Wet air
- 18 Rain and drizzle
- 20 Raindrops
- 22 Fog and mist
- 24 Frost and ice
- 26 Snowy weather
- 28 From breeze to gale
- 30 Under pressure
- 32 Superwinds
- 34 Twisters
- 36 Hot weather
- 38 Dry weather
- 40 Monsoon
- 42 A warm front
- 44 A cold front
- 46 Thunder and lightning
- 48 Colours in the sky
- 50 Changing weather
- 52 Pollution
- 54 Weather lore
- 56 Weather forecasting
- 58 The day
- 60 Index
- 61 Acknowledgements

What is weather?

Weather is just the way the air around you changes all the time. It can be still, moving, hot, cold, wet, or dry. Most importantly, weather is the way water changes in the air. Without water, there would be no clouds, rain, snow, thunder, or fog. The weather plays a big part in our lives and affects many of the things that we do.

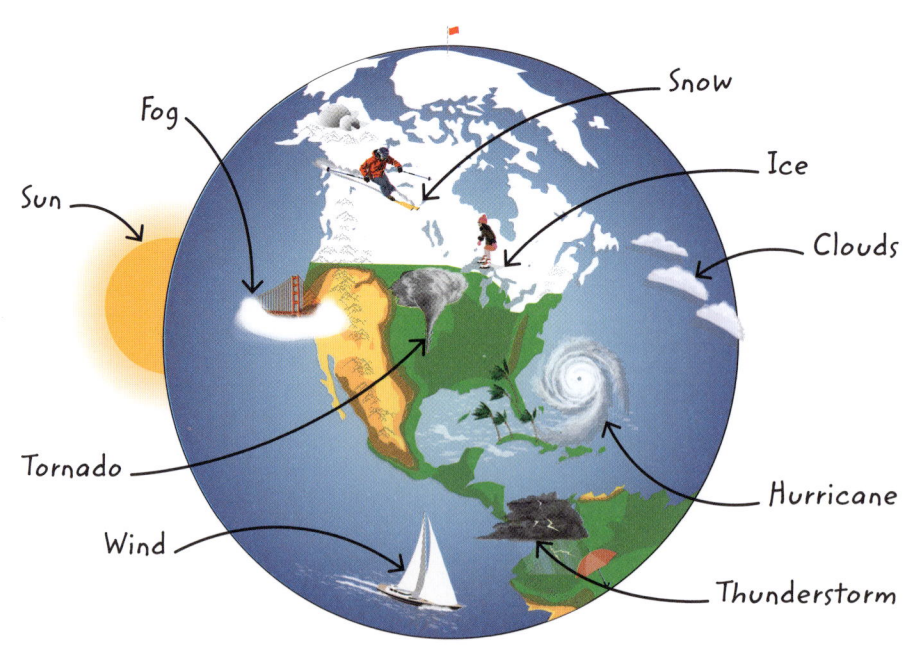

- Snow
- Fog
- Ice
- Sun
- Clouds
- Tornado
- Hurricane
- Wind
- Thunderstorm

Weather places
Weather is different in different parts of the world. In deserts, for instance, it very rarely rains, while in tropical jungles, it is hot and steamy. Climate is the usual kind of weather that a place has over a long period. For example, the Arctic has a cold climate.

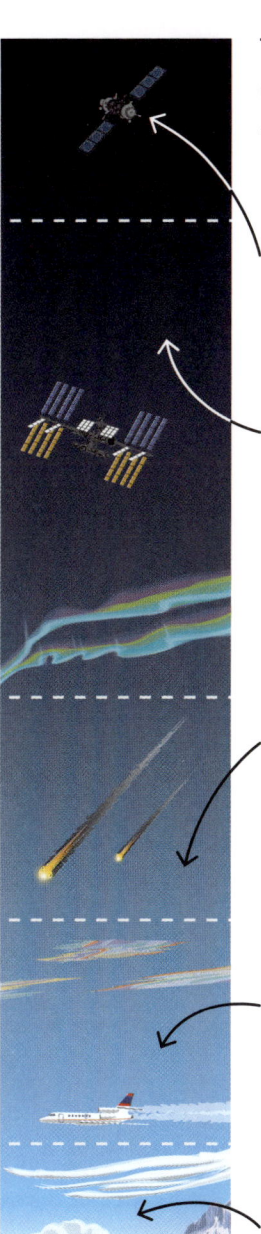

The atmosphere
Our planet is surrounded by a thin blanket of gases called the atmosphere. Weather only happens in the very lowest layer, the troposphere.

Satellites are stationed in the exosphere, 1,000 to 500 km (620 to 310 miles) from Earth.

The thermosphere is between 500 and 85 km (310 and 53 miles) from Earth. Here, you'll find the aurora lights and the International Space Station.

The mesosphere is between 85 and 50 km (53 and 31 miles) from Earth. Some of the ozone layer and meteorites are found here.

The stratosphere is between 50 and 12 km (31 and 7 miles) from Earth. Nacreous clouds sometimes appear in the lower level, and passenger planes often fly this high.

All our weather happens in the troposphere.

Weather forecasts
Weather experts use satellites to help them make more accurate forecasts. This satellite photograph shows a hurricane over an ocean.

The Ancient Greeks used to think that wind was the Earth breathing in and out. Now we know it is simply air on the move.

The seasons

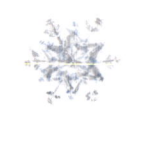

You can expect a certain kind of weather at certain times of the year. Winter days are often bitterly cold or stormy, while summer days may be warm and sunny. It all depends on the season. Some places have just two seasons, a wet one and a dry one. Other places have four: spring, summer, autumn, and winter.

Spring
Once winter is over, the Sun climbs higher in the sky, and the days get longer. Nights are cold but days can be warm.

Winter
Winter is the coldest time of year. The days are so short and the Sun hangs so low in the sky that the air barely warms up.

Hot Christmas
Because of the way the seasons work, winter happens in the United States when it is summer on the opposite side of the world, in Australia.

Cold winters bring snow.

Flowers grow in summer sunshine.

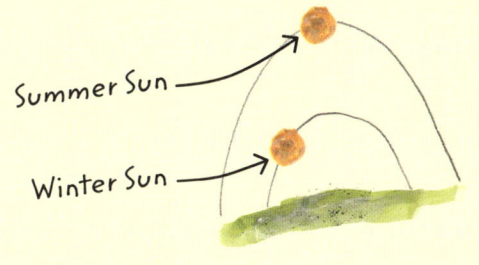

High and low
The seasons occur because the amount of sunlight reaching you varies. In summer, you will see that the Sun is much higher than in winter. This means that your part of the Earth is tilting towards the Sun.

Summer
The Sun is high in the sky at noon, and days are long and warm. Hot weather may be broken by thunderstorms.

Autumn
During autumn, the nights get longer and cooler again. Mornings are often misty. Sometimes they are frosty.

Autumn usually brings mists.

Winter sleep
Many animals, such as dormice, sleep away the winter to save energy. This is called hibernation.

The three clouds

Clouds come in all kinds of shapes and sizes, but they are all made of billions of tiny water droplets or even ice crystals floating in the sky. There are three basic types – wispy "cirrus" clouds, fluffy white "cumulus" clouds, and huge blankets of "stratus" clouds.

Cirrus clouds
Feathery cirrus clouds form very high up in the sky. It is so cold up there that they are made not of water droplets, but of tiny ice crystals.

Cirrus clouds high up in the sky often signal bad weather.

Mare's tails
Cirrus clouds are often called mare's tails, because strong winds high in the air blow them into wispy curls – just like the tail of a horse.

What makes a fluffy cloud?

Cumulus clouds form when sunshine warms up bubbles of moist air and causes them to rise quickly. As they get higher, they swell and are cooled so that the moisture turns into a mist of water droplets.

This cloud's fluffy shape shows how the bubble of warm, moist air billows out.

Cumulus clouds

Fluffy cumulus clouds are the clouds you usually see in fine weather, when the sky is blue. They look like heaps of cotton wool and are always changing shape. They are about 500 m (1,640 ft) above you.

Stratus clouds build up when warm, moist air rides up slowly over a bank of colder air.

Stratus clouds

The word "stratus" means "layers" in Latin, but you rarely see the layers in a stratus cloud. You just see a huge grey sheet of low cloud that can stretch for hundreds of kilometres.

Cloudspotting

Clouds come in many shapes and sizes – some large and fluffy, some small and wispy. It all depends on whether they are formed from water droplets or ice crystals. Weather experts identify clouds by how high they are in the sky, and whether they are layered (stratus) or in heaps (cumulus).

Cirrostratus
Clouds that form very high in the sky always start with the word "cirro". Cirrostratus clouds are made of ice crystals.

Altostratus
Medium-height clouds start with the word "alto". Altostratus is a layer of cloud made of water droplets.

Nimbostratus
These thick layers of cloud start near the ground and can be very tall. They can bring hours of rain or snow.

Stratus
Thick layers of stratus cloud hang close to the ground. Sometimes the Sun can be seen through them, looking like a silver disc.

Cirrocumulus
These tiny balls of icy cloud often form what is called a "mackerel sky", because they look like the scales of a mackerel fish.

Cirrus
Cirrus tend to be the highest clouds of all. They form streaks across the sky that tell of strong winds blowing. They are a sign of unsettled weather.

Altocumulus
These are medium-height cumulus clouds. They look like flattened balls of cotton that are almost joined together.

Cumulonimbus
These are the towering clouds that give us thunderstorms and even tornadoes. A big one may be taller than Mount Everest!

Cumulus
Fluffy cumulus clouds are easy to spot. These low-level clouds sometimes develop during the day and get bigger, giving showers.

Stratocumulus
If you see long rolls of these medium-height clouds, this usually means fair weather is on the way. They are made by cumulus clouds spreading out in layers.

Wet air

You might not know it, but you're sitting in a sea of water. Like a sponge, air soaks up invisible water vapour. All air contains water vapour, but how much it holds – the air's "humidity"– depends on how hot and dry it is where you are.

Wet breath
When you breathe out, you fill the air with water vapour. If the air is very cold, the vapour turns into millions of tiny water droplets and your breath looks "steamy".

Dew wonder
If air cools down, it can hold less water. After a cool night, leaves and grass are often covered in drops of water, or dew, that the air could not hold.

Dew drops

THE WATER CYCLE

Rain is the same water going round and round in a never-ending circle called the water cycle.

High up, water vapour turns into drops of water. This is called "condensation".

Big clouds are so full of water that some falls to the ground as rain.

Some rainwater seeps through the ground before reaching rivers.

1. Damp air
Water gets into the air because the Sun heats up oceans and lakes. Millions of litres of water then rise into the air as invisible water vapour. This is called "evaporation".

2. Falling rain
When some clouds get big, the droplets of water in them bump into each other and grow. They get so big that they fall to the ground as rain. This is called "precipitation".

3. Running away
Some rain falls straight into the sea. Rain falling on the ground fills up rivers and streams, which run back to the sea, then the cycle begins all over again.

Rain and drizzle

Without clouds, it wouldn't rain. Rain is simply water falling from clouds of tiny water droplets. Clouds form because air currents carry air up until it cools, and the water vapour turns into drops of water, which fall as rain. When the raindrops are very fine, they fall as drizzle.

Record rainfall
The wettest place in the world is Mawsynram village in India, where up to 11,872 mm (467 in) of rain falls every year.

Raining ice
Sometimes rain falls as solid chunks of ice, called hailstones. These are made when raindrops are tossed high up in huge clouds, and freeze into ice. As they are bounced up and down inside the cloud, they grow into big hailstones.

See how the ice builds up in layers, like the layers of an onion.

Base of large grey thundercloud, full of water

Rain approaching

This picture shows a heavy rainstorm over the Grand Canyon in the United States. Short, heavy showers like this are common in warm places, because the warmth can make air rise rapidly to create big rainclouds.

Weather clue
According to some country folk, you know rain is on its way when cows are all lying down in a field. Unfortunately, the cows sometimes get it wrong!

Raindrops

Every cloud holds millions of water droplets and ice crystals. They are so tiny that they are held up by air alone. Some big clouds have water droplets at the bottom and ice crystals at the top. Before rain falls, the droplets grow much bigger. Some grow by bumping into one another and joining together. Others grow by condensation.

See how they grow
In clouds forming high in the sky, water vapour freezes onto ice crystals, and they grow into snowflakes. Then they fall from the cloud. As they fall through warmer air, they melt into raindrops.

Tiny water droplets bump into each other and cling together as they fall.

Drop by drop
As a raindrop falls, it gathers up smaller ones below, growing all the time. The biggest raindrops are about 5 mm (0.2 in) across. But drizzle measures less than 0.5 mm (0.02 in) across.

Raindrops send up a splash of water. However, drizzle does not make splashes on water.

MAKE A RAIN GAUGE

If you want to keep a record of how much rain falls, why not make yourself a simple rain gauge like this? You will need a large plastic soft drink bottle, scissors, sticky tape, a measuring jug, a heavy flower pot, a notepad, and a pencil.

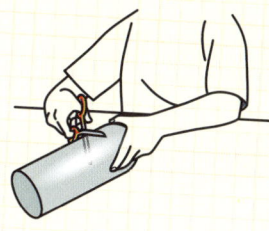

1. With an adult present, use a pair of good scissors to cut the neck off the bottle. Set the neck to one side, but don't throw it away!

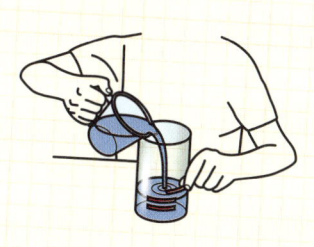

2. Use the measuring jug to pour 100 ml (3.5 fl oz) of water into the bottle. Mark the level with some tape and then pour in more water, marking each 100 ml (3.5 fl oz) until it is full.

3. Empty the water out and attach the neck of the bottle upside down to the bottom with tape.

4. Set your gauge outside in a heavy flowerpot (to stop it blowing over). Then every day, or week if you prefer, make a note of how much water there is in the bottle, using the marks to help you.

Every time you measure the water, you can plot the result on a graph.

Fog and mist

On a clear day, you can see for miles if you are high enough. But at other times the air may be so thick with fog that you can barely see across the road. Fog and mist look like smoke, but they are just tiny drops of water floating in the air. In fact, they are clouds that have formed at ground level.

Morning mist

Mist is made in the same way as fog, but is not as thick as fog. It clings close to the ground, and you can see over the top of it. Long, clear autumn nights often bring misty mornings – especially in valleys, because cold air drains down into a valley during the night.

Mist is thickest just above the ground, because it is the ground that cools the air.

Golden mist
San Francisco's Golden Gate Bridge is often wrapped in mist because the warm California air is chilled by cold ocean currents.

Night fog
It gets foggy when the air is too cool to hold all its moisture, or water vapour. At night when the sky is clear, the ground gets cold. It cools the air close to it, making water droplets form in the air. The thickest fogs form when the air holds a lot of moisture.

Fog cuts visibility (the distance you can see) to less than 1,000 m (3,280 ft).

Souper fog
Dust and smoke make fog much worse. Before coal fires were banned in London in the 1950s, the city had some of the world's worst fogs, called "peasoupers" because they were so thick and yellow-green!

Frost and ice

In winter, the days are short and the Sun hangs low in the sky, so we barely feel its warming rays. On clear nights, there is no blanket of clouds to keep in even this warmth. In some countries, it gets so cold that moisture in the air freezes, covering the ground with sparkling frost.

Pretty cold!
If you live in a country where it gets very cold, you may see lovely patterns of fern frost on your windows. This is made when tiny water drops on the glass turn into ice. As more moisture freezes on top of these icy drops, feathery fingers of frost begin to grow.

When moisture in the air freezes, it becomes frost.

Frosty nights
On cold nights, plants may get so cold that moisture in the air freezes onto them instantly, instead of forming liquid dew. This is called hoar frost.

Rime frost only forms on one side.

Ice needles
If fog forms in very cold air, the tiny water droplets that make up the fog freeze onto anything they touch. The ice builds up in thick layers called rime. This is often swept into strange shapes by the wind.

Winter fun
It is lucky for us that ice floats on water. When it is really cold, ponds, lakes, and canals are covered with a layer of ice. If ice sank, not only lakes but all the sea would slowly turn into solid ice!

Ice is frozen water.

⚠️ Never walk or skate on ice unless an adult has checked it is safe first!

Snowy weather

High up where the air is below freezing, clouds are made up of tiny ice crystals. These crystals grow into large snowflakes, which drift downwards and melt if the air gets warmer nearer the ground. However, if it is near or below freezing all the way down to the ground, we get snow instead.

White blanket
Once snow has covered the ground, it may not melt for a while, because the white snow reflects warming sunlight. If it melts and then refreezes, the crisp blanket will last even longer.

It snows the most when the temperature is at freezing point, which is 0°C (32°F).

Winter sports
Snowy weather can have its benefits! Skiing and tobogganing down a snow-covered slope are popular winter sports.

SNOW WONDER

Put some snowflakes on a coloured surface and look carefully at them under a magnifying glass. You will see that they all have a six-pointed shape. However, just as no two people are exactly the same, no two snowflakes are identical.

You'll have to work quickly before they melt!

Actual size of a snowflake.

Snowflakes look like delicate lace.

All sorts of snow

When it is below freezing, snow is powdery and "dry" and is useless for making snowballs! However, when the temperature is just about freezing, the snow is "wet" and easily crushed into heavy snowballs.

Igloos are dome-shaped houses built of solid blocks of snow.

"Wet" snow makes good snowballs.

From breeze to gale

Winds are simply the air around us moving. Sometimes the air moves so slowly that the wind is too weak to lift a feather. At other times, it moves so fast that trees and walls are blown down. Strong winds can be very dangerous. The Beaufort wind scale divides winds into 13 "forces". On the Beaufort wind scale, 0 is calm and 12 is a hurricane.

Clouds sweep across the sky

Force 2: Light breeze
When a light breeze blows, the weather is usually clear. You can feel air on your face, hear leaves rustle, and see plumes of smoke gently drifting.

Force 5: Fresh breeze
During a fresh breeze, clouds often start to scud across the sky, and small trees sway. Crested waves form on lakes.

Force 7: Near gale
During a near gale, the sky may be dark and stormy. Large trees sway and it becomes hard work walking against the wind.

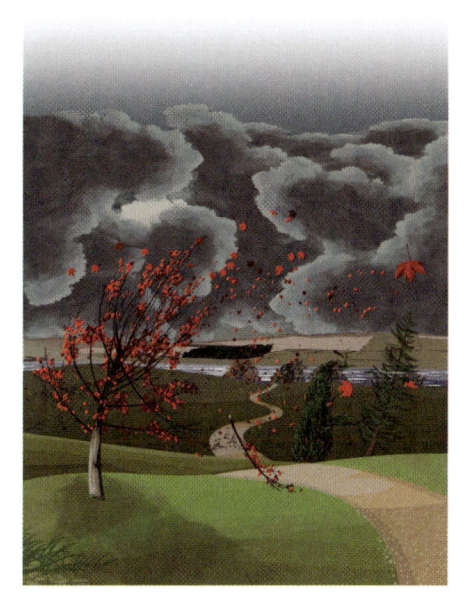

Force 9: Strong gale
When the wind blows at strong gale force, the sky may be covered in thick cloud. Large branches snap and chimneys and roof tiles can be blown off.

Wind power
Windmills were once used to grind corn. Now they are used to make electricity. Forests of windmills like these can make enough electricity to light a whole town.

Under pressure

You can't feel it, but the air is pushing down on you all the time. This push is called air pressure. Sometimes pressure is high; sometimes it is low. Changes in air pressure bring changes in the weather and make winds blow.

Ups and downs

Changes in air pressure are measured on an instrument called a barometer. When pressure is low, the weather is often wet and cloudy. When it is high, the weather is usually dry and clear.

When the air pressure drops, stormy weather is on the way.

This barometer measures pressure in units called hectopascals (hPa), which are the equivalent of millibars (mb).

When air pressure stays high, the weather is likely to stay fine.

MAKE A BAROMETER

This barometer will help you predict the weather. Make it on a rainy day when the air pressure is low, or it will not work. You will need a jam jar or straight-sided glass, a long-necked bottle, water mixed with food colouring, and a marker.

1. Set the bottle upside down in the jar so that it rests on the rim. The top of the bottle should not quite touch the bottom of the jar.

2. Take the bottle out and pour enough coloured water into the jar so that it just covers the neck of the bottle when it is in place. On the jar, mark the level of the water in the bottle.

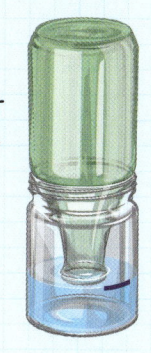

3. Set your barometer in a place where the temperature is fairly constant. Mark any changes in the water level over the next few weeks.

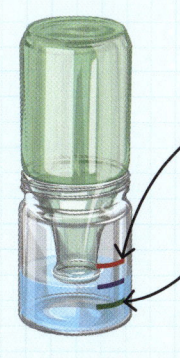

When the water is high in the bottle, pressure is high and it should stay fine.

When the water is low in the bottle, pressure is low and you can expect storms.

Right windy

Because the world is spinning, winds spin too – out of high and into low-pressure areas. Try standing with your back to the wind. If you live north of the equator, high pressure will be on your right. South of the equator, it will be on your left.

Superwinds

In summer, tropical places are hot and sunny. During autumn, the skies darken and storms sweep in from the sea, bringing fierce winds and lashing rain. These storms are called hurricanes, typhoons, or tropical cyclones, depending on where you live.

Tropical revolving storm
A hurricane starts when hot tropical sunshine stirs up moist air over the sea. It then whirls over the ocean in a giant spinning wheel of cloud, wind, and rain.

Picture of a hurricane taken from a satellite in space

Blown away
Howling hurricane winds can do terrible damage. On the coast, huge waves raised by the winds can swamp the shore.

Hurricane slice

What goes on inside a hurricane? Fierce winds hurtle around the bottom of the storm, but the centre is dead calm. The air that spirals up around the centre builds up tall rain clouds.

Warm, damp air spirals up around the centre of the storm, making huge clouds.

Hurricanes may be 1,500 km (932 miles) across and 12 km (7 miles) or more high. Hurricane winds in the Northern Hemisphere spin in the opposite direction to the hurricane winds in the Southern Hemisphere.

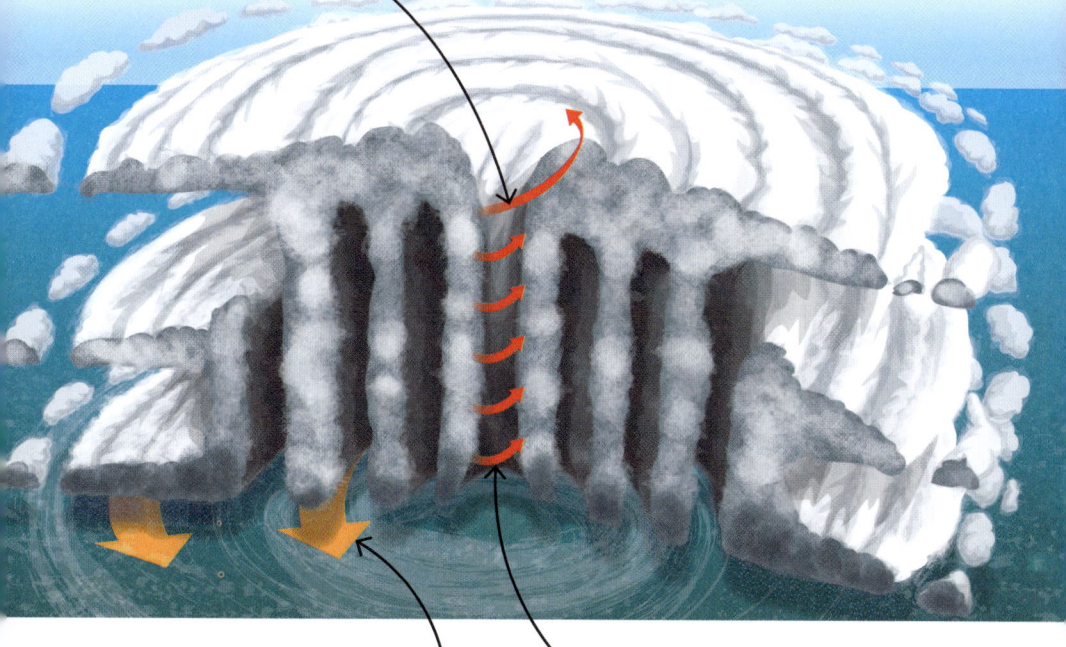

Hurricane winds blow around the base of the storm at 300 kph (186 mph) or more.

The air in the very centre, or "eye", of the storm is clear and calm.

Every hurricane is given a name. Once, only girls' names such as Jane and Diana were used, but now they use boys' names too.

Twisters

Twisters, or tornadoes, are whirling funnels of air. They hang down from thunderstorm clouds, which form in very hot and humid weather. Twisters usually last about 15 minutes, but if the bottom of a funnel touches the ground, it will smash everything in its path instantly.

Twisters are like the funnel that forms when water is sucked down a plughole.

Twister alert

If you see thunderclouds with small, rounded "lumps" beneath them, they are a good sign that a tornado is on the way. These bulging clouds are called mammatus clouds.

White column

Inside a tornado, air is sucked upwards and starts to spin at enormous speed. An approaching tornado is white, because it has not yet touched the ground and picked up dust and debris.

Waterspout
When a tornado develops over calm seas, it is called a waterspout. Mist, spray, and water are sucked up into the twisting funnel.

Tornadoes are most common in the United States.

On target
A tornado makes a deafening roar as it passes by. As the bottom of a tornado touches the ground, it sucks dust and debris high into the sky. It can also lift heavy objects before hurling them back to the ground.

At the centre of a tornado, wind speeds can reach 400 kph (250 mph). They are the fastest winds on Earth.

Hot weather

In places where the Sun sits high in the sky at midday, the days are long and the weather is hot. Hot weather often comes with high pressure areas, because they bring clear skies and light winds. High pressure can last for a long time, making hot, sunny weather last for days on end.

Mirage
Sometimes, on a very hot day, you may see a mirage – a pool of water on the road ahead. Then, as you approach, it disappears. What you are actually seeing is the reflection of the sky on a layer of hot air just above the ground.

Thermometer
Thermometers help us to measure the temperature. Sealed inside a glass tube is some dyed alcohol. The liquid expands as the temperature rises and shrinks as it gets colder.

Glass tube holding alcohol dyed blue.

THE POWER OF THE SUN
The Sun gives off energy, which we feel as heat. Its energy can be trapped by solar panels and made into electricity.

If the day starts sunny with few clouds, the temperature soon starts to rise.

The Sun is high in the sky.

Short trails of condensation are left by the aircraft.

"Heat-haze" is made when dust and pollution are trapped near ground level.

A hot, dry day
On a hot day, if the air is dry and calm, there are no clouds in the sky. Hot, humid weather is more unpleasant, because water vapour in the air makes us feel sticky and uncomfortable.

Dry weather

Some countries have plenty of water and shortages are rare. However, in some parts of the world water is scarce, and people can never be sure when it will rain next. Droughts happen when for months – or even years – on end, the Earth's surface loses more water than it collects. In some places, called deserts, rain hardly ever falls at all.

Drought
If droughts last for a very long time, animals die of thirst, crops wither in the hot Sun, and people have to go without food – they may even die of starvation.

Parched, cracked land

Desert scene
You'll often find deserts inland, next to mountain ranges. The mountains act as a shield and keep rain-bearing clouds away. Semi-deserts like this one in Arizona, in the United States, have a little rainfall – enough to support plants that can store water, like cacti.

In true deserts, plants and animals can only live near oases, which are areas of open water.

Death Valley
One of the driest and hottest places in the world is Death Valley, in the United States. People have died of thirst here in the extreme heat.

Not all deserts are hot. Central Antarctica is one of the driest places on Earth.

Dust Bowl
Drought can affect many people's lives. In the 1930s, The Great Plains of North America suffered from a disastrous drought that created a "dust bowl". Terrible dust storms buried crops and houses, and many people were forced to leave their homes.

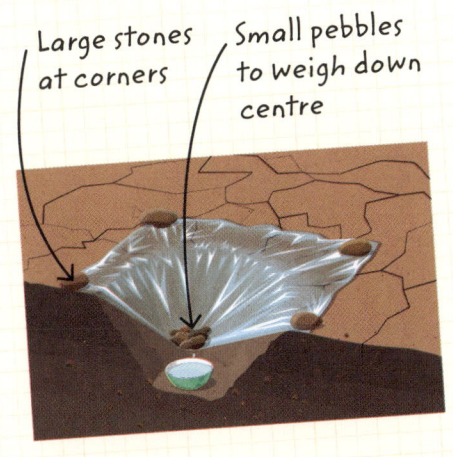

MAKE A GARDEN MOISTURE TRAP

Dig a hole and put a bowl in the centre. Cover it with plastic, held down by stones. The next day, you'll see water in the bowl. This happens because water evaporates from the soil and condenses on the plastic, running off into the bowl.

Large stones at corners

Small pebbles to weigh down centre

Monsoon

A monsoon is a seasonal wind that blows for about six months in one direction, then turns around and blows in the other direction for six months. In summer, moist winds from the ocean bring dark, rain-bearing clouds to the land. In winter, the cycle is reversed. Wind blows the air from the land to the sea, bringing cool, dry weather.

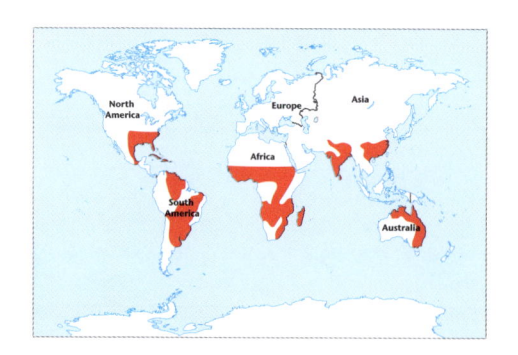

The monsoon areas are coloured red.

Where the wind blows
The monsoon is best known in Asia, but monsoon winds also bring rain to other places in the tropics including Africa, South America, the southern United States, and Australia.

Before the monsoon
During the early summer, the hot Sun heats up the dry tropical land, while the seas and oceans stay cooler. As warm air rises above the land, cool, moist air from the sea rushes in to fill its place. The winds blowing the sea air bring heavy rainfall.

Life goes on
The rain is often so heavy that it washes away crops and floods the streets. Violent thunderstorms can also occur, but whatever the monsoon brings, life goes on.

Monsoon in action
Monsoons are vital for growing crops. Once the monsoon begins, the wet conditions are ideal for rice farmers, who can start planting young rice plants in the flooded fields.

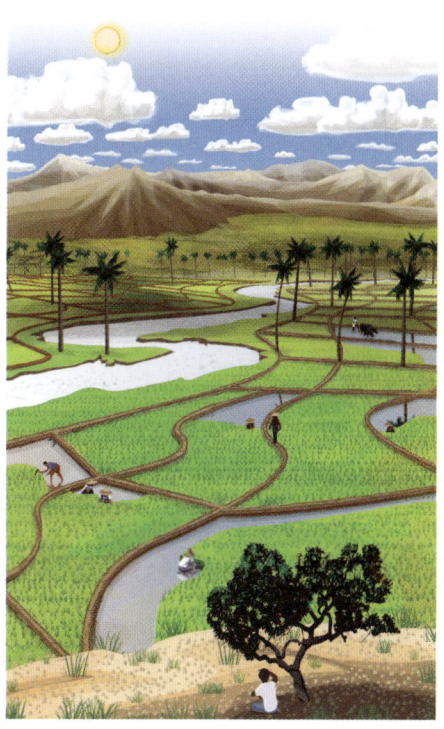

After the rain
For six months, showers sweep across the land. Finally, the wind and rain die down. The cool air flows back towards the sea and the land begins to dry.

A warm front

If weather forecasters say a "front" is on the way, then expect the weather to become wet and windy. A warm front is where a mass of warm moist air is pushed up over a mass of colder, drier air creating clouds and rain. Fronts move along with areas of low pressure, and the winds blow stronger as they pass by.

Wispy warning
When you see wisps of feathery cirrus clouds in the sky, you can be sure a warm front is on the way.

Clouding over
After a while, the sky gets hazy and the clouds thicken. Fluffy altocumulus clouds appear, looking like streaks of cotton wool. The wind grows stronger, making the sea very choppy.

Nimbostratus clouds

Wet and windy
Soon the sky is dark with thick nimbostratus clouds. It begins to rain steadily and goes on raining for several hours. If it is cold enough, it may even snow.

Red line
On weather maps, a warm front is a line with red bumps on it. The bumps point the same way as the wind blows.

A cold front

Fronts usually come in pairs. Often there is only a brief gap between one front passing and the next arriving. The first is a "warm" front because it brings warmer air. The second is a "cold" front, and brings colder air and sometimes even stormier weather than the warm front.

Stratocumulus clouds bring occasional drizzle.

On the move
On a weather map, a cold front is a line with blue spikes. The spikes show which way the cold air is moving.

Brief relief
As the warm front moves away, the rain (or snow) stops and it gets warmer. Near the coast it stays cloudy, and there may be drizzling rain.

In summer, inland, the Sun comes out and it can get hot after the warm front has moved away.

Storm overhead

You know the cold front is on its way when the wind becomes stronger, giving gusts that rattle windows. The sky may fill with huge dark thunderclouds that lash the countryside with rain or even hailstones.

More rain may fall in the few minutes a cold front passes than all the hours of a warm front!

The sea is very rough.

It's all over

The worst of the storm is soon over. It feels colder as the clouds clear, leaving a blue sky with fluffy cumulus clouds. However, there may still be more violent showers to come.

The sea is calmer.

Thunder and lightning

Hot, sticky summer days often end in violent thunderstorms. Dark, towering thunderclouds send forks of lightning flashing across the sky, and booming thunderclaps fill the air. The electricity from just one bolt of lightning could light a small town for a whole year!

Flash and crack
Inside a storm cloud, violent winds swirl snow, hailstones, and rain up and down. Electricity builds up in the cloud and escapes as a flash of lightning.

Lightning flashes between the bottom of the thundercloud and the ground.

Lightning and thunder happen at the same time, but you see the lightning first because light moves faster than sound. Thunder is the sound of air bursting as it is heated rapidly by lightning.

Strike

Lightning always takes the quickest path to the ground. So tall trees and buildings are most likely to be struck. The world's tallest buildings are struck by lightning hundreds of times each year.

Each fork of lightning is many lightning flashes running rapidly up and down the same path.

You can work out how far away a storm is by counting the seconds between a flash of lightning and a thunderclap. For every three seconds you count, the storm is 1 km (0.6 miles) away.

Holy thunder

Some Native Americans believed that the sacred thunderbird made thunder by beating its enormous wings, and that lightning flashed from its beak.

Colours in the sky

The sky isn't always blue, even when it's fine. Near sunset it can be purple or even red. This is because sunlight is made up of the seven colours of the rainbow, all jumbled up together. As sunlight bounces in different ways off dust and other particles in the air, different colours appear.

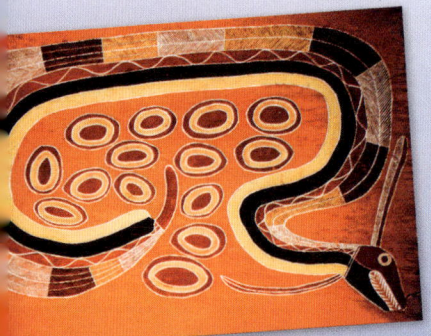

Rainbow Snake
Australian Aboriginals worship a spirit known as the Rainbow Snake. He lives in water and is the great creator who has made the features of the Earth. He can appear as a rainbow.

Rainbows are curved because of the way light hits the round raindrops.

Curving colours
When sunlight passes through raindrops in the air, the light splits into seven colours – red, orange, yellow, green, blue, indigo, and violet. Many raindrops help to create the pattern.

Ring around the Sun
When the Sun shines through thin icy cloud, a coloured halo may appear. This is caused by ice crystals in the cloud splitting sunlight into the seven colours, just as raindrops do. Never look directly at the Sun, as it will damage your eyes!

MAKE A RAINBOW
You can make your own rainbow with just a glass of water and bright sunlight. Stand the glass on white paper, facing the Sun. The sunlight will shine through the glass and split into the seven colours.

You always see the colours in a rainbow in the same order, from red through to violet.

Sometimes there is a second, outer bow, and its colours are always the other way round.

To see a rainbow, the Sun must always be behind you.

Changing weather

The world's weather has changed many times. About 10,000 years ago, great sheets of ice covered a third of the Earth. That was the last Ice Age. Today we live in a much warmer climate. Many scientists think we have harmed the atmosphere so much that the world is getting even warmer.

Prehistoric weather

Millions of years ago, when dinosaurs roamed the land, much of Europe and North America was covered in forests. The climate was hotter and more humid than it is today.

Sun trap

Only a small portion of the Sun's heat reachs the Earth. But the Earth stays warm because gases, such as carbon dioxide, trap the heat — just like the glass in a greenhouse. Carbon dioxide is a greenhouse gas that is made when we burn wood, coal, or oil. If we produce too much, the Earth may get too warm.

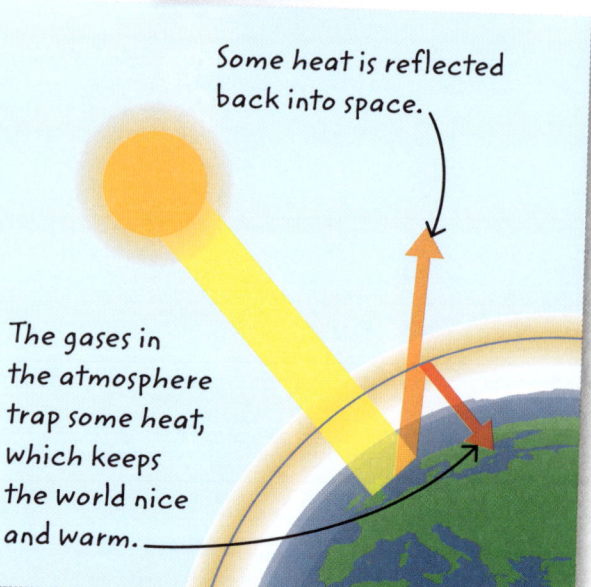

The gases in the atmosphere trap some heat, which keeps the world nice and warm.

Some heat is reflected back into space.

A big umbrella

When volcanoes erupt, they throw large amounts of dust and smoke high into the atmosphere. This cuts off sunlight, shading the ground like a big umbrella. This can make temperatures drop all over the world for a year or more.

Save the trees

Trees take in carbon dioxide and release oxygen and moisture, which is turned to rain. Cutting down the trees stops them doing this, and burning them releases all the carbon dioxide they soaked up as they grew, helping to raise the Earth's temperature.

Tropical rainforests are vital in removing excess carbon dioxide from the air. But in the Amazon region, an area of rainforest the size of Britain is cut down ever year for farming.

Pollution

You may find it hard to believe, but many things people do every day create pollution. Too much pollution can cause changes in the weather. It may get too hot in some places, and cause floods or drought in others. Cutting down on pollution now means a cleaner world tomorrow!

Pollution problems
Smoke and gases from factories pollute the air and may form smog. This is a mixture of smoke and fog, which can make people sick. Car exhausts may give off poisonous gases that not only affect our lungs but can block out the sunlight.

Acid rain
Power stations that burn coal or oil to generate electricity release waste gases into the air. The gases drift on the wind until raindrops dissolve them, making "acid rain". This eats away at buildings and kills trees, plants, and life in rivers and lakes.

Acid rain, carried by wind, can destroy pine forests thousands of kilometres away.

TEST FOR ACID RAIN

Here is an experiment you can try to test for acid in rainwater. You will need two finely chopped red cabbage leaves, distilled water (from a pharmacist), rainwater, a bowl, two glass jars, a measuring jug, and a sieve.

1. Put the leaves into the bowl. Get an adult to pour hot distilled water over them. Then let them stand for an hour.

2. Strain the cabbage juice into a measuring jug. The liquid should be a dark purple colour.

3. Pour 20 ml (0.7 fl oz) of distilled water into one jar, and 20 ml (0.7 fl oz) of rainwater, collected from your garden, into the other.

4. Add the same amount of cabbage juice to each jar. The water will change colour. Compare the colour of the distilled water (this stays the same) and the rainwater. If the rainwater turns red, it is acidic.

Rainwater

Distilled water

The stronger the acid, the redder the water gets.

The Earth's blanket

The ozone layer of our atmosphere protects us from the Sun's harmful ultraviolet rays. However, some chemicals can destroy it. As a result, holes have appeared in the ozone layer, allowing more of the harmful rays to reach the Earth's surface and damage many living things.

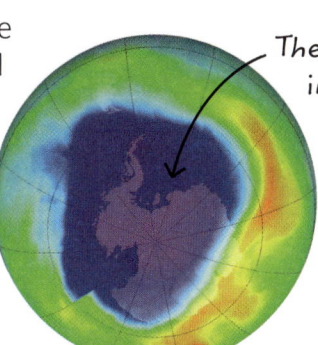

The blue areas in this satellite photograph show the hole in the ozone layer over the Antarctic.

Weather lore

Nowadays, weather forecasters use satellites and radar to tell us what the weather holds. Before this, people used to look for clues in nature to predict the weather. They didn't just look at the skies – they also watched how animals and plants acted. Some of the signs are reliable, but others aren't foolproof!

Groundhog forecast
In the United States, people say that if you can see a groundhog's shadow at noon on the second of February, there will be six more weeks of winter. Fortunately, the groundhog isn't always right!

Red sky at night
People used to say a red sunrise meant bad weather to come, and that a red sunset meant good weather to come. Try to watch the sky at sunrise and sunset to see if this saying is always correct.

OPEN AND CLOSE

Pine cones are traditionally used to forecast the weather. Put a pine cone outdoors and watch what happens. It will open out in very dry weather and close up when it is damp.

The pine cone's scales open in dry weather.

Scales are tightly shut in wet weather.

Flower power

When you want to know what the weather will be like, look for the magic carpet flower. It grows in the wild in South Africa and is a popular garden plant elsewhere. The petals stay wide open in fine weather, but they close up when the sky grows dark.

Frog-cast

One way to tell if it's going to rain soon is to look out for frogs. They love to come out when it's damp. As the air usually becomes humid before it rains, you may see more frogs about and you will know to expect rain.

Weather forecasting

To work out what weather is on its way, forecasters take measurements from weather stations all over the world. They also study information gathered by satellites in space. The information is entered into powerful computers that work out how it might affect the atmosphere. The results are then used to forecast how the weather is going to change.

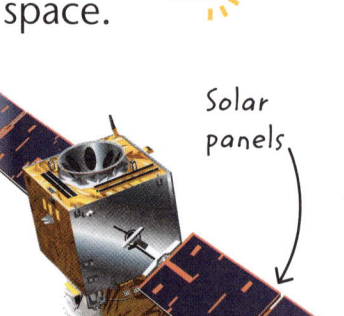

Solar panels

Weather satellite
Satellites in space are controlled by teams of people on Earth, but they can carry out many tasks automatically.

WEATHER SYMBOLS
Every type of weather has a special symbol. Try keeping track of the weather for a week and see how many different symbols you use.

- Sunny
- Sunny intervals
- Cloudy
- Light rain
- Heavy rain
- Thundery showers
- Hail showers
- Heavy snow

Weather map

Information about the weather is often shown on maps. Places where the atmospheric pressure is the same are joined by lines called isobars. The isobars form rings around zones of low pressure and high pressure.

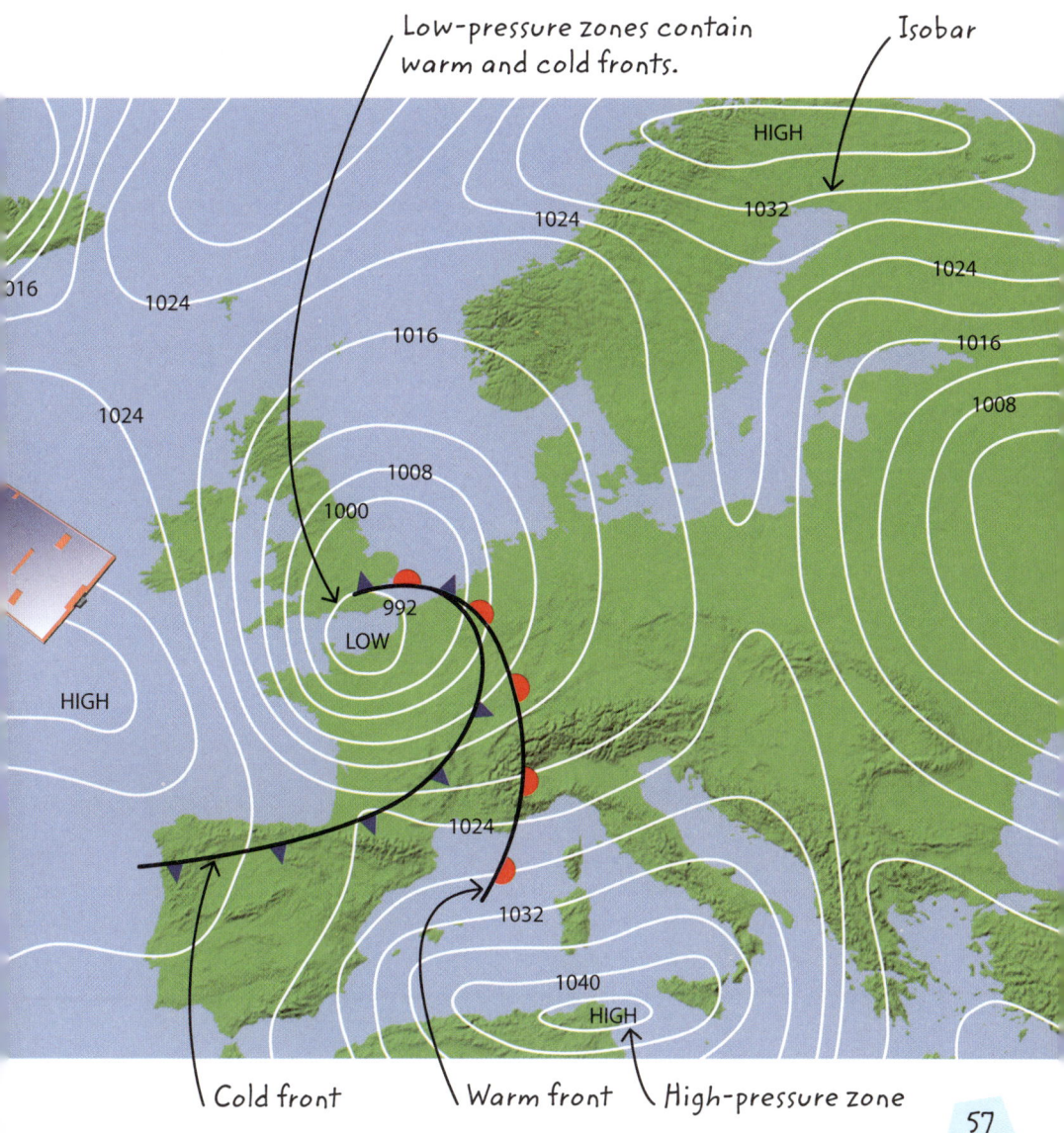

Low-pressure zones contain warm and cold fronts.

Isobar

HIGH
1032
1024
1024
1016
1016
1024
1008
1024
1016
1008
1000
992
LOW
HIGH
1024
1032
1040
HIGH

Cold front   Warm front   High-pressure zone

57

The day

During the course of each day there are changes in the weather. On fine days, you can almost tell the time by the way the weather changes through the day – from the cool chill of dawn through the heat of the afternoon to the clear, calm evening.

Sun rise
Dawn is usually chilly, as the ground loses heat steadily all night. It is often misty too, for the cool of the night makes water condense in the air.

Midday
As the Sun climbs in the sky, morning mists fade away and it gets warmer. By midday, a few fluffy cumulus clouds appear, made by rising warm, moist air.

Mid-afternoon
Mid-afternoon is the warmest time of the day. Often, though, the morning's fluffy cumulus clouds can build up and up until they interrupt the afternoon with brief but heavy showers of rain, or even thunderstorms.

Towards sunset
As the Sun drops lower towards sunset, its power to stir up the air gets less and less. So the end of the day is often calm and clear, with barely a cloud in the sky.

Night
Once the Sun has dropped below the horizon it gets steadily colder – especially if there are no clouds to keep the heat in.

Index

A
acid rain 52–53
air 8–9
air pressure 30–31, 57
altocumulus clouds 15, 42
altostratus clouds 14
atmosphere 9, 50–51
autumn 11

B
barometers 30–31
Beaufort wind scale 28–29
breezes 28

C
carbon dioxide 50, 51
cirrocumulus clouds 15
cirrostratus clouds 14
cirrus clouds 12, 42
climate 8
climate change 50–51
clouds 12–15, 34, 42, 43, 44, 45, 58–59
cold fronts 44–45, 57
colours, rainbow 48–49
condensation 17, 20, 58
cumulonimbus clouds 15
cumulus clouds 13, 15, 45, 58, 59

DE
deserts 8, 38–39
dew 16, 24
drizzle 18, 20
drought 38–39, 52
dry weather 38–39
dust bowl 39

exosphere 9

F
floods 41, 52
fog 22–23, 25, 52
fog and mist 22–23
forecasts 9, 54–55, 56–57
frogs 55
fronts 42–43, 44–45, 57
frost 24–25

GH
gales 29
greenhouse gases 50
groundhogs 54

hailstones 18, 45, 46
heat-haze 37
high pressure 30, 31, 36, 57
hoar frost 24
hot weather 36–37, 38–39
humidity 16, 37, 55
hurricanes 9, 32–33

IL
ice 24–25
Ice Age 50
isobars 57

lightning 46–47
low pressure 30, 31, 57

MN
mackerel sky 15
magic carpet flower 55
mammatus clouds 34
mare's tails 12
mesosphere 9
mirages 36
mist 22–23
moisture trap 39
monsoon 40–41

nimbostratus clouds 14, 43

OP
ozone layer 9, 53

pine cones 55
pollution 52–53

R
rain 17, 18–19, 20–21, 56
rain gauge 21
raindrops 20
rainbows 48–49
rainforests 51
rime frost 25

S
satellites 9, 56
seasons 10–11
showers 19, 45, 56, 59
smog 52
snow 20, 26–27, 46
solar power 36
spring 10
storms 45, 46
stratocumulus clouds 15, 44
stratosphere 9
stratus clouds 13, 14
summer 11
Sun 10–11, 14, 17, 24, 36–37, 38, 40, 44, 50, 52, 58–59
sunset 48, 54, 59

TV
temperature 36, 50–51
thermometers 36
thermosphere 9
thunderstorms 15, 34, 45, 46–47, 59
tornadoes 15, 34–35
tropical cyclones 32
troposphere 9
twisters 34–35
typhoons 32

volcanoes 51

W
warm fronts 42–43, 44, 57
water 8
water cycle 17
water vapour 16–17, 18, 20, 23, 37
waterspouts 35
weather maps 43, 44, 57
wind 9, 28–29
wind power 29
winter 10, 11, 24–25, 26–27

Acknowledgements

Dorling Kindersley would like to thank:

Carl Gombrich, Gin von Noorden and Kate Raworth for editorial assistance and research.
Sharon Grant and Faith Nelson for design assistance.
Ron Lobeck for help with writing text.
Hilary Bird for the index.
Jim Sharp for help with authenticating text.

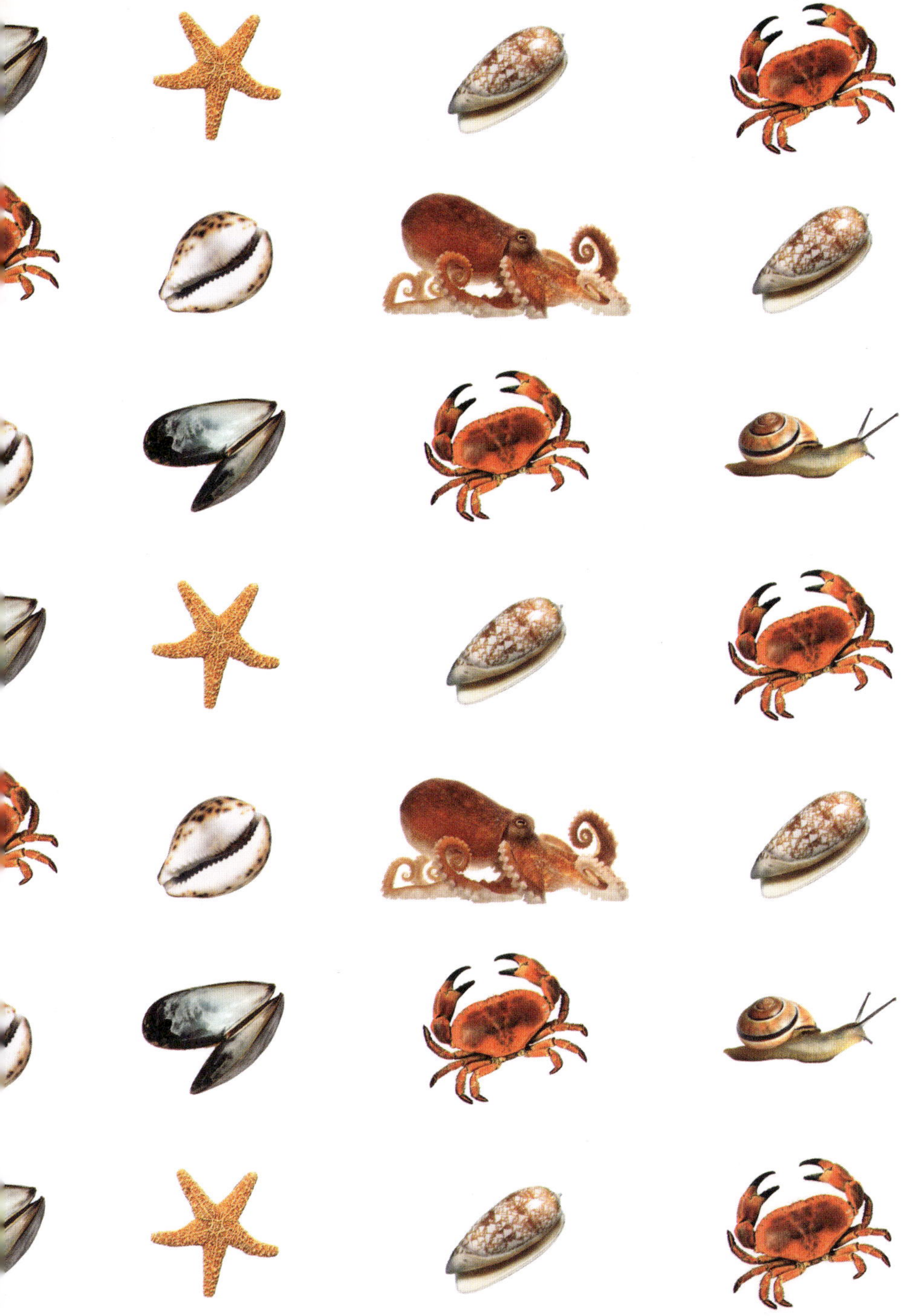

A shore crab will nip you if you step on it. So, walk carefully.

A seahorse uses its tail to anchor itself to plants.

Deadly spines on fins

Lionfish are brightly coloured.

Sharp spines

Sea urchins cling to the rock with hundreds of tiny sucker-tipped feet.

Seashore

Written by David Burnie
Consultant: John Woodward

DK

DK Penguin Random House

Senior editor Gill Pitts
Editors Radhika Haswani, Olivia Stanford
Editorial assistance Cécile Landau
Senior art editor Ann Cannings
Art editor Kanika Kalra
Illustrators Abby Cook, Dan Crisp, Shahid Mahmood
Jacket co-ordinator Francesca Young
Jacket designers Dheeraj Arora, Amy Keast, Faith Nelson
DTP designers Sachin Singh, Dheeraj Singh
Picture researcher Sakshi Saluja

Senior producer, pre-production Nikoleta Parasaki
Producer Isabell Schart
Managing editors Soma B. Chowdhury, Laura Gilbert, Monica Saigal
Managing art editors Neha Ahuja Chowdhry, Diane Peyton Jones
Art director Martin Wilson
Publisher Sarah Larter
Publishing director Sophie Mitchell

Original Edition
Editor Claire Bampton
Art editor Rebecca Johns
Project editor Mary Ling
Production Catherine Semark
Editorial consultant Kathie Way
Illustrators Nick Hewetson, Tommy Swahn, Peter Visscher
Picture researcher Diana Morris

First published in Great Britain in 1994.
This edition first published in Great Britain in 2017 by
Dorling Kindersley Limited
80 Strand, London, WC2R 0RL

Copyright © 1994, 1997, 2017 Dorling Kindersley Limited
A Penguin Random House Company
8 7 6 5 4 3 2 1
001–308947–Nov/2017

All rights reserved.
No part of this publication may be reproduced, stored in or introduced into a retrieval system, or transmitted, in any form, or by any means (electronic, mechanical, photocopying, recording, or otherwise), without the prior written permission of the copyright owner.

A CIP catalogue record for this book is available from the British Library.
ISBN: 978-0-2412-8253-3

Printed and bound in China.

The publisher would like to thank the following for their kind permission to reproduce their photographs:
(Key: a-above; b-below/bottom; c-centre; f-far; l-left; r-right; t-top)
4 Dorling Kindersley: Natural History Museum, London (bl). **8 Dorling Kindersley**: Paul Wilkinson (cl). **8-9 Dorling Kindersley**: Stephen Oliver (t). **9 Dreamstime.com**: Pockygallery11 (tr, cr). **15 Dorling Kindersley**: Natural History Museum, London (cr). **18 Dreamstime.com**: Yael Weiss (tl). **22 Alamy Stock Photo**: David Pick (b). **Dreamstime.com**: Mikelane45 (tr, cr). **23 Alamy Stock Photo**: Karen van der Zijden (b); ZUMA Press, Inc. (tl). **24 123RF.com**: guy ozenne (ca). **25 Getty Images**: Despite Straight Lines (Paul Williams) (clb); Science Photo Library (cla). **26 Dreamstime.com**: Eugene Kalenkovich (bl). **27 Robert Harding Picture Library**: Frank Hecker / Okapia (bl). **28 Dreamstime.com**: Mario Pesce (bl). **29 Alamy Stock Photo**: Blickwinkel / Hecker (cl). **34-35 Dorling Kindersley**: Natural History Museum, London (b). **39 Dorling Kindersley**: Linda Pitkin (tl). **FLPA**: D P Wilson (r). **40 123RF.com**: Jolanta Wojcicka (bl). **41 123RF.com**: Krzysztof Odziomek (crb). **Dorling Kindersley**: Natural History Museum, London (cla). **42 123RF.com**: Andrzej Tokarski (cl); Vitalii Hulai (cra). **43 Dorling Kindersley**: Jan Van Der Voort (crb). **45 Alamy Stock Photo**: Blickwinkel / Hecker (br). **46 Dorling Kindersley**: Linda Pitkin (cr). Dreamstime.com: Asther Lau Choon Siew (bl). **47 123RF.com**: Sergdibrova (tl). **Dorling Kindersley**: Linda Pitkin (br). **54 Dorling Kindersley**: Twan Leenders (br). **55 123RF.com**: Joe Quinn (c); Vasiliy Vishnevskiy (cra). **57 123RF.com**: Tiero (c). **58-59 Alamy Stock Photo**: Carolyn Clarke (b). **59 Alamy Stock Photo**: FLPA (cra). **Dreamstime.com**: Brett Critchley (crb). **Getty Images**: Glowimages (br)

Cover images: **Front**: 123RF.com: Vitalii Hulai (tc); **Back**: Dorling Kindersley: Natural History Museum, London (cla)

All other images © Dorling Kindersley
For further information see: www.dkimages.com

**A WORLD OF IDEAS:
SEE ALL THERE IS TO KNOW**
www.dk.com

Contents

- 8 The seashore
- 10 What shapes the shore?
- 12 Making waves
- 14 Tides and tidal zones
- 16 Signs in the sand
- 18 Beach detective
- 20 High and dry
- 22 Just visiting
- 24 Shell shapes
- 26 Borers and burrowers
- 28 Seashore fish
- 30 Look carefully
- 32 Underwater garden
- 34 Holding on
- 36 Life adrift
- 38 Making a meal
- 40 Danger, keep clear!
- 42 Life in the dunes
- 44 Sandy shore
- 46 Coastal corals
- 48 Shingle beach
- 50 Rocky shore
- 52 Rock pool
- 54 Muddy shore and salt marsh
- 56 Mangrove swamp
- 58 Harbour and pier
- 60 Index
- 61 Acknowledgements

The seashore

It's fun at the seaside! In warm weather, it is a good place to keep cool, and there is always lots to do and see. In this book, you can find out about seashore plants and animals, and explore the different types of coasts.

Exploring the shore
You can find out a lot about seashore wildlife without any equipment at all, but you will discover even more if you have a dip net.

Always ready
Some seashore animals are stuck to rocks, so they cannot run away. This makes them easy to study. Other animals are always on the alert for danger and will run or swim away if they see you coming.

Crabs scurry away sideways!

Hide and seek
Part of being a seashore explorer is knowing where to look for animals. This spiny squat lobster will hide under a stone when the tide is out.

Keeping a notebook

A notebook helps you to remember what you have seen on the shore. Drawing something is a good way of finding out exactly how it is shaped. You don't have to be a wildlife artist to keep a notebook, but with practice you might turn into one!

★ Remember to record exactly where, and at what time of the year, the seashore animal was found. Always put animals back where you found them!

What shapes the shore?

The shore is always on the move. In some places, the sea eats away at the land, so the shore moves back. In other places, it builds up banks of sand or shingle, so the shore moves forwards towards the sea. By knowing what to look for, you can see these changes at work.

Wave power
When waves smash against a cliff, water is forced through cracks in the rock.

Natural arch formed by waves.

Stack

Crumbling rock
In time, the rock breaks apart. Sometimes, it leaves a hole which widens to form an arch.

Collapse
The rock arch gets wider and wider, until one day it collapses into the sea. All that is left is a tall, rocky stump, called a stack.

Graded grains

When the sea attacks a rocky shore it breaks up the rock and then pushes the pieces along the coast. It can move heavy boulders only a short distance, but it can carry sand a long way. The pebbles shown here were collected at regular intervals along a 20-km (12-mile) coastline.

Rocks are rounded into large pebbles by the pounding waves.

Large pebbles break up to make smaller ones.

Coarse pebbles are small enough to roll around in the waves.

The motion of the waves wears the pebbles away to shingle.

The pebbles eventually break up to make sand.

MAKING A SHORE PROFILE

If you draw part of a shoreline, you can see where the shore is changing. Cliffs and rocky stacks show where the shore is being eaten away. Level shingle and mud often show that the shore is building up.

Making waves

Waves are made by the wind. When the wind blows over the ocean, it pushes and drags against the surface. The surface starts to ripple and waves form. Waves can travel huge distances. A storm can whip up waves in one part of an ocean, but many hours may pass before they reach the shore.

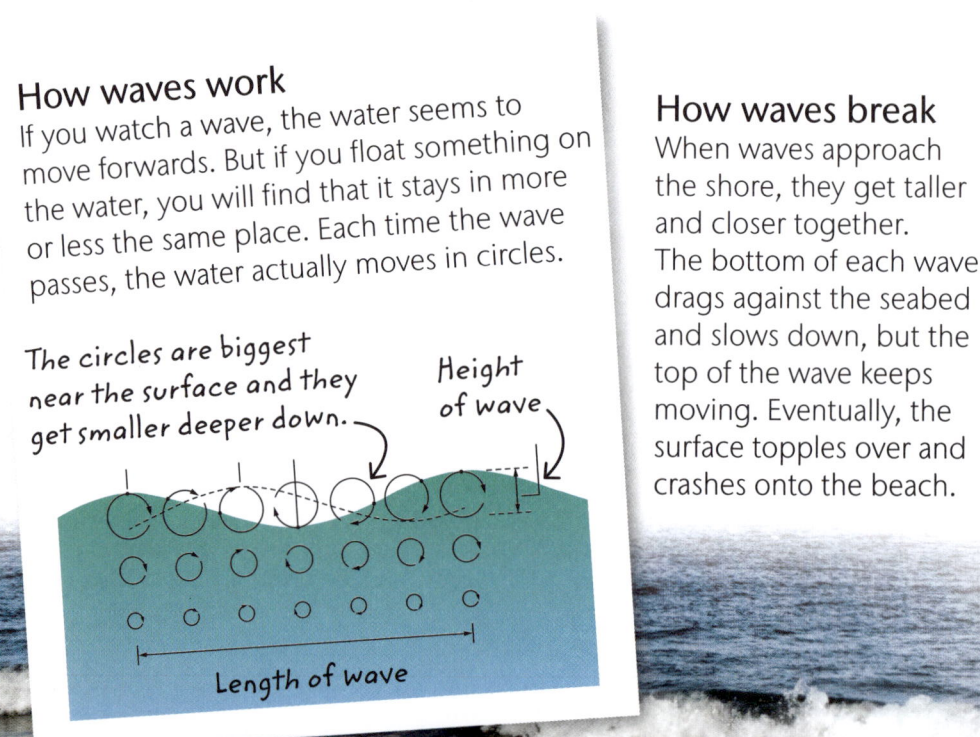

How waves work

If you watch a wave, the water seems to move forwards. But if you float something on the water, you will find that it stays in more or less the same place. Each time the wave passes, the water actually moves in circles.

The circles are biggest near the surface and they get smaller deeper down.

Height of wave

Length of wave

How waves break

When waves approach the shore, they get taller and closer together. The bottom of each wave drags against the seabed and slows down, but the top of the wave keeps moving. Eventually, the surface topples over and crashes onto the beach.

Waves on the turn

Waves normally travel in straight lines. But if part of a wave enters shallow water, it slows down. The rest of the wave keeps moving as before, so the whole wave turns.

Here you can see how waves change direction as they pass an island. Behind the island the waves meet head on.

MAKING A PAPER BOAT

To make your own paper boat, you will need a square piece of paper.

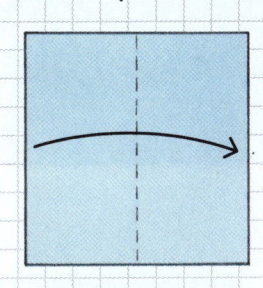

1. Fold the piece of paper in half.

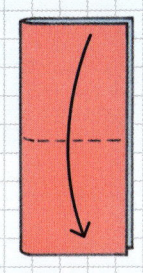

2. Fold the paper in half again, from top to bottom.

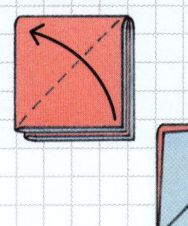

3. Fold the top sheet of paper backwards to form a triangle.

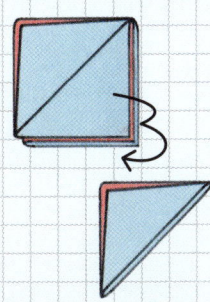

4. Fold the other three sheets of paper in the opposite direction.

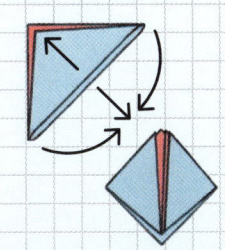

5. Pull open the triangle into a cup and fold it together to form a square.

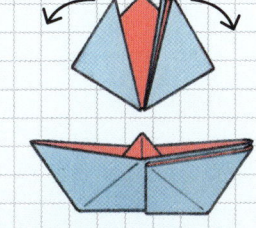

6. Gently pull out on the two halves to get your boat ready to sail.

Tides and tidal zones

The world's highest tides are found in the Bay of Fundy, between Canada and the United States. The sea level can rise or fall by the height of a four-storey building in just six hours! However, even small tides have an important effect on shore wildlife.

When the Sun and Moon are in a line with the Earth, tides are extra high.

What causes tides?
Gravity causes tides. The sea is held in place by the Earth's gravity. The gravity of the Sun and Moon tugs at the Earth's seawater and pulls it towards them.

Zones on the shore
Some seashore animals and plants need to be in water all the time. Others can survive for a while in air, when the tide is out. This means that the wildlife is arranged in zones.

Oarweed grows in or below the lower shore.

Starfish usually live below the level of the lowest tide.

Shore crabs can live in and out of water.

Subtidal zone

Lower shore

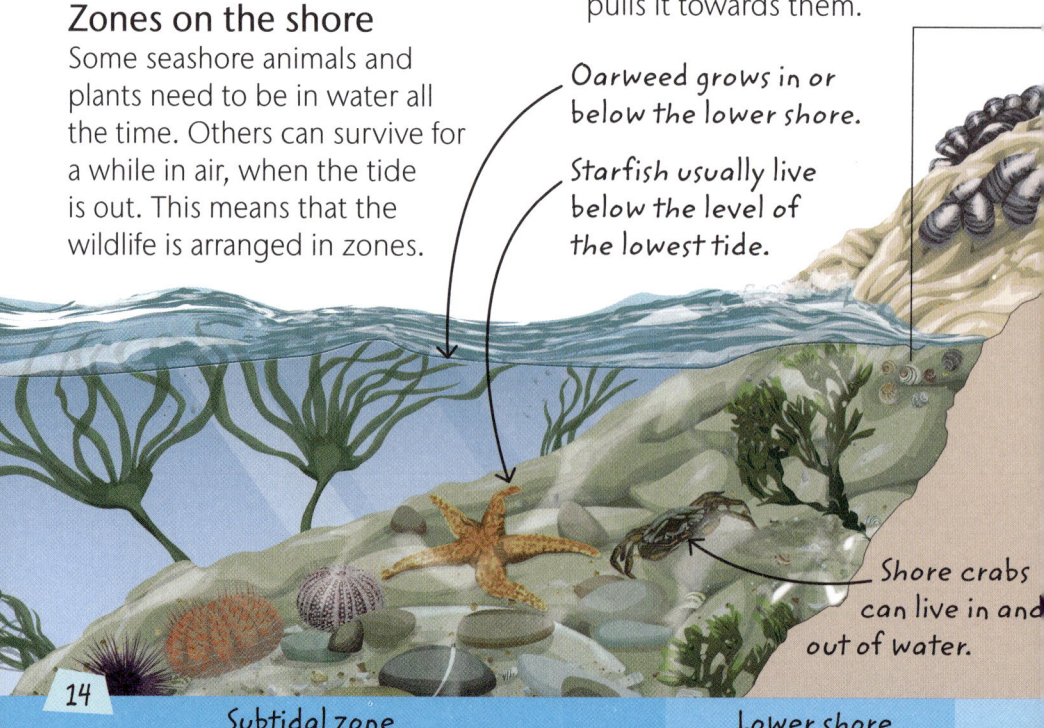

Making a profile

On some shores, the zones are easy to see. You can keep a record of them by making a shore profile showing what kinds of plants and animals live at different levels. See if you can spot the very highest barnacle on a rocky shore.

Topshells live on the middle or lower shore.

Mussels close up at low tide to stop themselves from drying out.

Time for a meal

When the tide falls, many seashore birds come to the water's edge looking for small animals, stranded as the water level drops.

Oystercatchers use their long beak to dislodge limpets.

Rock pipits feed all over the shore above water.

Sea lettuce grows in pools in the middle and upper shore.

Periwinkles wander high into the splash zone.

Prawns will die out of water.

Limpets can survive in air for a long time.

Middle shore | Upper shore | Splash zone

Signs in the sand

A sandy or muddy shore is a perfect place for spotting tracks. When the tide falls, it leaves a smooth, damp surface. Animal feet sink in as they walk over the sand or mud, leaving a tell-tale trail of footprints.

Gull tracks
A gull has three forward-pointing toes. The middle toe is straight, but the other two are curved. The toes are connected by flaps of skin called webs, which help the gull to swim.

A gull walks with its feet turned slightly inwards.

Going for a run
A dog's paws have four small pads near the front and a larger pad at the back. If the dog is running, its claws leave deep marks in the sand.

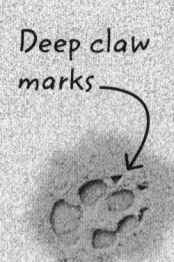

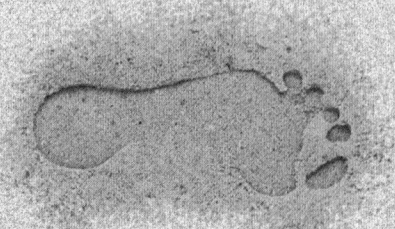

Deep claw marks

Feet on the beach
The depth of your footprints, and the distance between them depend on how fast you are moving. When you look at footprints on the beach, see if you can work out whether the person that left them was walking or running.

When someone is walking, they leave an even footprint.

Four-toed tracks

Cormorants usually live on rocks, but sometimes they leave tracks on sandy or muddy beaches. A cormorant foot has four outward-pointing toes, joined by a web of skin. All its toes are straight and the front toe is the longest.

Webbed toes

Heron tracks

Herons have three forward-pointing toes and one toe that points backwards. They hunt by wading into the water and they often leave tracks on muddy sand. Herons have a long stride, so their footprints are wide apart.

Cormorants have short legs, so their footprints are close together.

Backward-pointing toe

When someone is running, their toes leave more of a mark than their heels.

A human footprint is narrowest in the middle, where the foot arches.

Beach detective

Every day, the sea throws all kinds of objects onto the shore. These include shells, seaweed, and even old coins. For a beach detective, the best place to start investigating is the strandline – the line of "leftovers" washed up by the tide.

Hidden danger
The animals that live in these cone-shaped shells have powerful stings. Don't touch them!

Dead shells lose their colour

A live starfish has flexible arms, but a dead one is stiff.

Stranded starfish
If a starfish is washed up on the beach, it will dry out and die. Its dry body then takes a long time to break down.

Driftwood often looks like bones or even animals.

Sea smooth
Pieces of wood are worn smooth by the sea.

Weed out of water
After a storm, seaweed is dislodged and thrown high up onto the beach. This bladderwrack has dried and become stiff.

Coral treasure
In warm parts of the world, you may see pieces of colourful coral.

Urchins are covered with spines when they are alive.

Shell fragment

The sea keeps beach sand on the move and grinds up shells and stones.

No spines
Sea urchin shells are very fragile (weak) and they quickly get broken up by waves.

Pieces of glass

Cockle shells in two halves

Cone shell with short, pointed spine

Beach bones
Skulls are good for detective work, because they show how an animal lived. This skull belonged to a brown pelican that fished with its huge beak.

Long, flattened beak

Not everything on the beach is natural. Plastic does not decay in the sea and plastic bottles and bags can float across the oceans.

High and dry

For humans, cliffs can be dangerous places, so be careful when you go on a clifftop walk. However, for some animals, cliffs are places of safety. Seabirds breed on cliffs because their enemies cannot reach them there. For a few weeks every year, some sea cliffs are home to many noisy birds, jammed tightly together on every rocky ledge.

Miniature mine
A sandy, sheltered slope makes a perfect nest site for a cliff mining bee. The female bee digs out a branching tunnel. She stocks each side branch with some pollen and lays an egg in it.

Free flight
Gulls use the breeze over cliffs to lift themselves up, so they can stay in the air without flapping their wings. By adjusting the slant of its wings, a gull can hover and look for food.

Birdwatcher's paradise
Cliffs are wonderful places for birdwatching, particularly if you have a pair of binoculars. In spring and early summer, lots of birds set up home on different parts of the cliffs. In autumn and winter, many birds leave for the open sea.

Clowns of the clifftops
It is easy to recognize a puffin, because it has a stripy beak and bright red feet. Puffins nest in burrows, which they dig in clifftop turf. They often stand at the entrance to their burrows, cleaning their feathers and flapping their stubby wings.

Noisy neighbours
Kittiwakes nest on high rocky ledges. They make their nests from seaweed glued together with droppings. Kittiwakes often nest in huge numbers and their shrieking calls fill the air.

Life on a ledge
Guillemots do not make nests. Each female lays a single egg on a rocky ledge and stands guard over it. One end of the egg is very pointed, so that it can only roll around in a circle. This makes it less likely to fall over the edge.

Ground floor
Cormorants nest at the bottom of the cliffs, just above the waves. They lay eggs in seaweed nests. Cormorants often stand with their wings open, drying their feathers in the breeze.

Just visiting

In many parts of the world, the seashore is visited by different animals at different times of the year. In winter, many birds fly in from colder places far away. In spring and summer, the shore is a place where animals raise their young. Summer is also when humans flock to the coast for their holidays.

Summer visitors
Have fun at the seaside, and remember – when you go home, leave nothing behind but your footprints!

Pink-footed geese migrate along the coast.

Homing in
The coast is a good winter home for birds, as it is usually warmer than places further inland.

Thief in the night
In warm parts of the world, the small Asian mongoose visits the shore after dark. It eats crabs and other seashore animals, and it also sniffs out turtle eggs buried in the sand. When it finds a turtle's nest, it digs up the eggs and feasts on them.

Fish out of water
The California grunion is a fish that lays its eggs on land. Grunion gather close to the shore after dark and then wriggle onto the beach to lay their eggs. As soon as the grunion have finished, they return to the sea.

Coming ashore to breed
Seals spend most of their time in water, but they give birth on land. Seals do not like to be close to humans. They come ashore on remote parts of the coast, where they can raise their young without being disturbed.

A seal pup may remain on shore for three months, before entering the sea.

Joining in
Dolphins are very clever animals that are full of curiosity. They often swim just in front of boats and enjoy playing with humans. In some parts of the world, dolphins come close to the shore to be near swimmers.

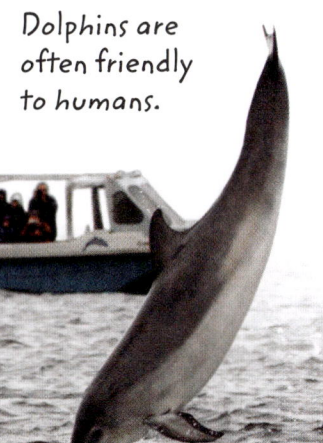

Dolphins are often friendly to humans.

Shell shapes

When you walk along a shore, you will find lots of empty shells. A shell is a special shelter that protects an animal from its enemies, and stops it drying out at low tide.

Cowries
A cowrie has a slit-shaped opening, lined with teeth like a comb.

Separated
Many shells have two hinged halves. After the owner dies, the two halves may soon become separated.

The top of the tightly coiled spire is the oldest part of this shell.

Olive shell
These shells look a bit like cones, but they are longer and thinner.

Wrap-around shell
A cone shell has an almost flat spiral at one end. The older the shell, the more turns its spiral has.

Corkscrew shell
Many shells have a long spiral at one end, like a corkscrew.

Smooth lining
Shells are often rough or bumpy on the outside, but inside they are usually very smooth.

Inside of shell is smooth and shiny.

The barnacles have a better chance of finding food if the shell's owner moves around.

This conch shell has been worn smooth by the sea.

Taken for a ride
The outside of a shell is often turned into a home by other animals or plants. Barnacles need a solid surface to live on and a shell suits them very well.

Going to pieces
After a sea animal dies, its shell is slowly worn away. Eventually, only tiny pieces will be left.

Seashells to keep
Shells like this scallop are fun to collect. Picking up empty shells does not harm wildlife, unlike buying shells in shops.

High rise
Slipper limpets grow in piles, with several shells stacked on top of each other.

It is worth sifting and sorting sand or shingle to find small shells like these for your collection.

Borers and burrowers

It's easy to dig a hole in the sand, but imagine being able to dig one through solid rock! Many seashore animals protect themselves by digging. Some live in rocks or wood, and others live in sand or mud.

Shell halves have rough edges.

Piddock's shell in rock

Burrowing in the sand
Tusk shells are molluscs that spend their lives in deep water, partly buried in sand. They collect food from the sand with their short tentacles. Their shells are often washed up on beaches.

Boring through rock
The two halves of the piddock's shell work just like a drill bit, turning one way and then the other, boring through soft rock.

Scraping out a home
Sea urchins use their spines and mouth parts to scrape a hollow shelter in solid rock. The spines are made of a mineral called calcite, which is similar to our teeth.

Sea urchins shelter in rock.

Hiding below the surface
Look carefully when you are walking at low tide for signs of worms below the surface. The sticky feeding tubes of the sand mason are easy to spot.

Waste piles up here.

Water, sand, and mud enter through one end.

Sand mason

U-tube
Mud and sand are perfect hiding places for animals with soft bodies. A lugworm lives in a U-shaped burrow. It swallows sand and mud that falls into the burrow's entrance, digesting any food that it contains. The lugworm then squirts waste out of the other end of the burrow.

Head

Tube of sand and small shells.

Lugworm's tail

Sinking the ship
Shipworms are not really worms at all, but molluscs. They use their shells to bore through wood, digesting wood flakes as they move along. When all boats were made of wood, shipworms were a serious pest.

Seashore fish

Many seashore animals stay in one place, so it is easy to get a close look at them. Watching fish is a bit more tricky. Fish are always on the alert and they will usually swim for cover if they see you coming.

Keeping upright

A seahorse is an unusual small fish that swims upright. Its body is covered with bony plates and it uses its tail to anchor itself to underwater plants. If you look at its head, you can see how it gets its name.

Fast mover

Blennies live in rock pools in many parts of the world. If you try to scoop one up with a net, you will find that it can change direction with lightning speed.

The butterfly blenny lives near the shore and in deep water.

Like most blennies, the tompot blenny has a long fin along the top of its body.

Finger-sized fish

Gobies are small fish that nearly always live in shallow water. They have large eyes and are quick to spot any sign of danger. This is a black goby, which is common on rocky coasts.

Its paddle-shaped tail fin helps the goby to swim.

Sand dweller

Dragonets bury themselves in sandy or muddy seabeds to hide from predators. They mostly eat worms, molluscs, and shellfish. Male dragonets are brightly coloured, while females are a dull brown.

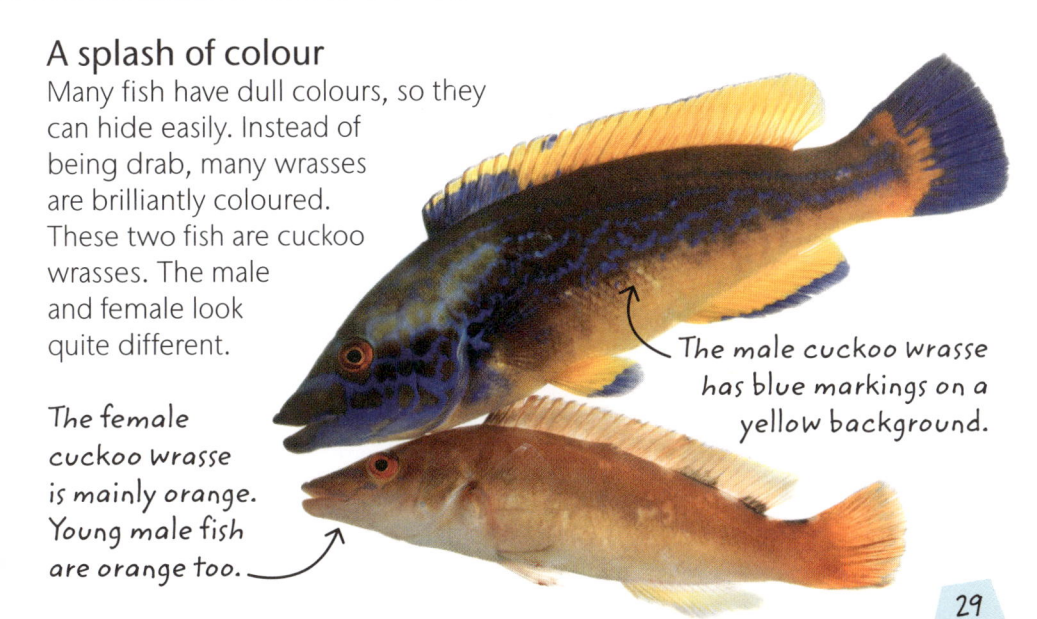

A splash of colour

Many fish have dull colours, so they can hide easily. Instead of being drab, many wrasses are brilliantly coloured. These two fish are cuckoo wrasses. The male and female look quite different.

The male cuckoo wrasse has blue markings on a yellow background.

The female cuckoo wrasse is mainly orange. Young male fish are orange too.

Look carefully

Life is not easy for seashore animals. They have to find enough to eat, but they also have to make sure that they do not get eaten themselves. Many avoid being seen by their enemies by having special shapes and colours that match their background.

Find that fish!
A pipefish has a very long body and is not much thicker than a pencil. It hides among underwater plants and sucks in pieces of floating food through its mouth.

Straight-nosed pipefish

You can only see the underside of a ray's body when it swims.

A perfect match
On the seabed there is nothing to hide behind. Flatfish and rays settle on the sand or gravel and have special markings that blend in with their background.

This ray has brown and white markings that look like the sunlit seabed.

A sole is a type of flatfish. Can you spot the other one buried in the seabed?

MAKING A SEASHORE MASK

To make your own disguise you will need a balloon, some newspaper, some sand, some shells, seaweed, half a cup of flour, and half a cup of water.

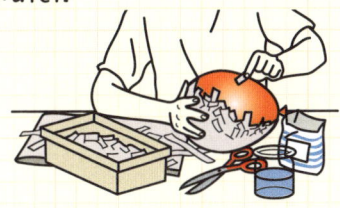

1. Mix flour and water to make a runny paste. Blow up the balloon. Glue layers of paper strips to the upper side of the balloon.

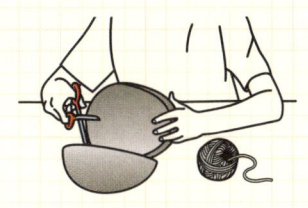

2. When the paper is hard and dry, lift the mask away from the balloon. If it is stuck, burst the balloon!

3. Ask an adult to help you cut out some eyeholes and add some shells, sand, and seaweed.

Wear the mask to disguise yourself.

Disappearing crab

The long-legged spider crab hides in seaweed and it even fastens small pieces to its body. Can you spot its claws and its long spidery legs?

Breathing tube of a buried masked crab

Underwater garden

One of the world's fastest-growing living things is giant kelp, a seaweed found off the coast of California. Seaweeds have flat fronds instead of leaves. They are useful hiding places for small fish. See how many you can find here!

Wracks often live in rock pools.

Brown seaweeds
Brown seaweeds grow at any depth. Wracks have narrow fronds. Kelps have broader fronds.

Green seaweeds

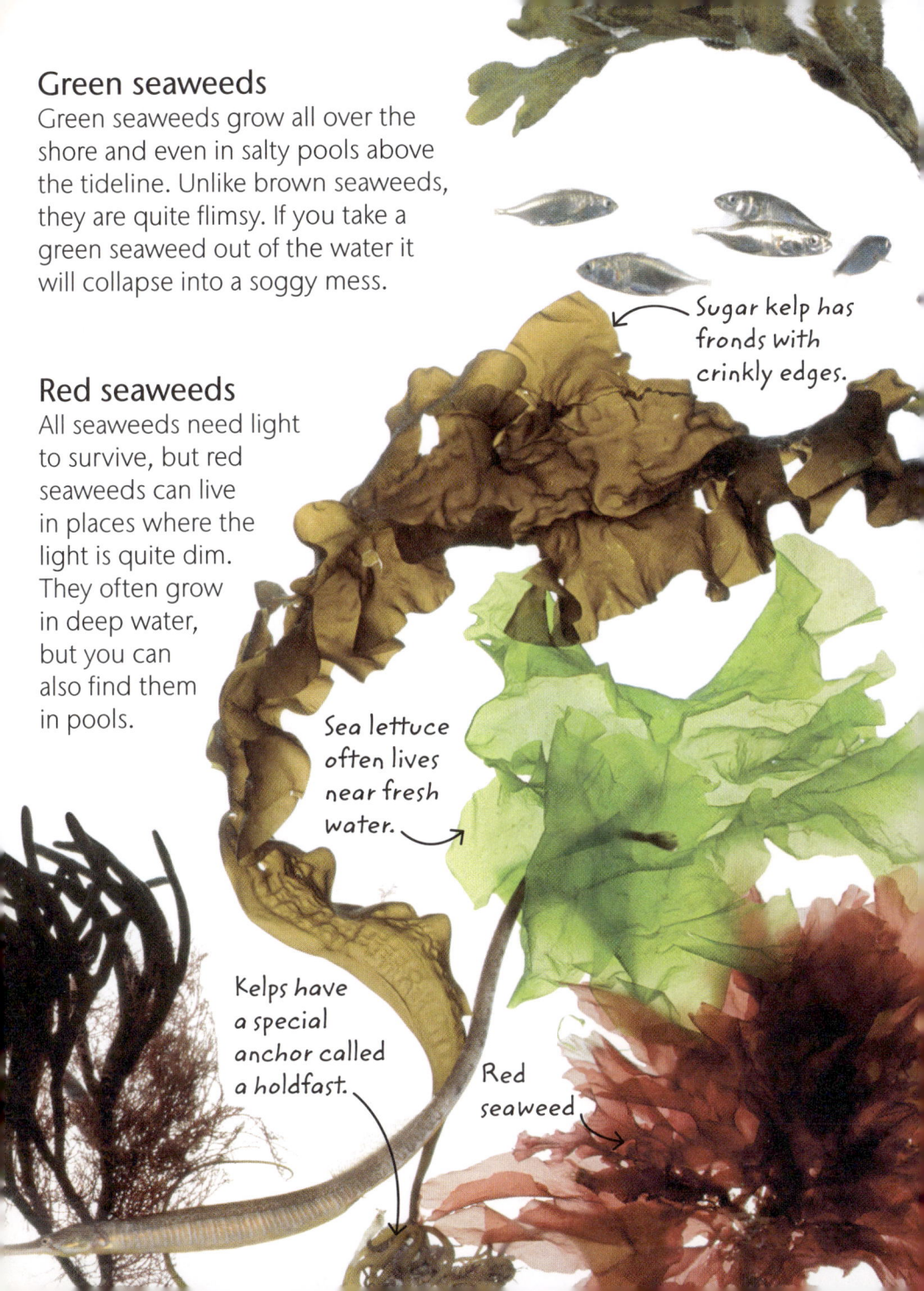

Green seaweeds grow all over the shore and even in salty pools above the tideline. Unlike brown seaweeds, they are quite flimsy. If you take a green seaweed out of the water it will collapse into a soggy mess.

Red seaweeds

All seaweeds need light to survive, but red seaweeds can live in places where the light is quite dim. They often grow in deep water, but you can also find them in pools.

Sugar kelp has fronds with crinkly edges.

Sea lettuce often lives near fresh water.

Kelps have a special anchor called a holdfast.

Red seaweed

Holding on

If you can imagine being out in a hurricane, you will know what it is like for seashore animals when the waves crash around them. Waves are very powerful and seashore plants and animals can only survive them by holding on tight. If they let go, they may be hurled against the rocks and torn to pieces.

A hanging egg
Dogfish are small sharks that lay their eggs close to the shore. Each egg has a rubbery case and special tendrils that wrap around seaweed. The tendrils hold the egg safely in place, while the young dogfish develops inside.

Stuck to a rock
Many rocky shore animals use special suckers to keep themselves in place. This sea anemone has fastened itself to a rock and extended its tentacles.

Sharp spines

Sea urchins cling to the rock with hundreds of tiny sucker-tipped feet.

Getting a grip
Seaweeds do not have proper roots, but they are good at holding on to rocks. Sometimes a seaweed fastens itself to a rock that is too small and light. If this happens, waves may pick up the rock and the seaweed and throw both of them onto the shore.

Sea anemone attached to hermit crab's shell

Crab on the move
The hermit crab uses its strong legs to hang on to rocks. If the crab is threatened, it often pulls its legs into its shell and drops into the safety of deeper water.

Hermit crab grips a rock.

Starfish cling on with tiny tube feet, just like sea urchins.

Riding on the storm
A limpet has a large, sucker-like foot that can clamp its shell on to the rock. Even powerful waves cannot budge it.

Limpet covered with algae

Life adrift

How many living things do you think there are in a bucket of seawater? About a dozen? A hundred? A single bucket of seawater can contain millions of living things. Together they make up "plankton" – a mass of life that drifts with the currents.

When they hatch, cod fry feed on plankton.

Fish fry
Cod release their eggs in the open sea and the eggs hatch into tiny "fry". Life is hard for these baby fish, and only a few survive.

Cased in glass
Diatoms are microscopic algae that float around in the sunlight. Each one is covered by a glass-like case.

Plant-like plankton
This strange plant-like object has long "horns" that help to stop it sinking.

Changing shape
When crabs are young, they often drift in the open sea. As they get older, they change shape and live on the seabed.

Trailing by
Like most seaweeds, this kelp is fixed to something solid on the seabed, so it cannot move about. However, some seaweeds float on the surface of the sea. They drift with the currents and provide a home for tiny animals.

Drifting jellies
Jellyfish spend their lives drifting with the tides and currents. Once a jellyfish is on land, its body collapses and it cannot move at all.

Long, feathery tentacles carry food to its mouth.

Slow progress
A jellyfish moves by tightening and relaxing its bell-shaped body. When the bell tightens, it pushes water backwards so that the jellyfish moves forwards. Jellyfish cannot swim very fast and they often get washed up on beaches.

Making a meal

In the sea, food is often all around. Most of this food is made of tiny particles that are smaller than a pinhead. Some seashore animals spend all their adult lives filtering out a share of this floating feast. Others get their food by hunting, or by bumping into it.

Eight-armed hunter

Octopuses hunt crabs and other small animals. An octopus will smother a crab with its long arms and then give the crab a venomous bite. Octopuses usually spend the day hidden in rocky crevices and they come out to feed after dark. They can change their skin colour to match their background, or to show what mood they are in.

An octopus swims by squirting a jet of water out of the base of its body.

Powerful suckers allow the octopus to grip and move quickly over the seabed.

The living submarine
Cuttlefish are relatives of octopuses and they catch their prey using tentacles. Inside its body, a cuttlefish has a special shell containing lots of tiny spaces. It can fill the spaces with fluid or gas so that it rises or sinks, just like a submarine. It swims by rippling its fins, or by shooting out a jet of water.

Long hunting tentacles are surrounded by shorter arms to form a protective shield.

Danger adrift
The Portuguese man-of-war drifts on the surface of the sea and has long stinging tentacles that trail many metres into the water. If the tentacles touch a fish, they paralyze it and then pull it upwards to be digested.

Filtering food
A sea squirt is a tiny animal shaped like a bottle with two openings. It sucks in water and filters out any particles of food. It then pumps the waste water out of the opening on its side.

Tentacles armed with thousands of tiny stings.

Water flows in here.

Water flows out here.

Sea squirts often live in groups.

Danger, keep clear!

When exploring the shore, remember that not everything likes to be touched or picked up. Most seashore animals are quite harmless, but some have sharp claws, or even venomous spines. A few have such powerful venom that they can kill or injure people.

Deadly spines on fins

Warning signs
Animals that are brightly coloured, like this lionfish, are often dangerous. The lionfish lives in warm coral seas. Its stripes show that it has venomous spines. The lionfish's venom is strong enough to kill a human.

The fire coral's bright yellow colour warns that it is dangerous.

Coral attack
All corals catch their prey by using stinging threads. The fire coral's threads can pierce human skin and cause a lot of pain.

Nasty nip
A shore crab will nip you with its pincers if you accidentally step on it. It might hurt, but some shore animals are much more dangerous.

Danger in the sand
The weever is a fish with venomous spines. It is hard to spot as it partly buries itself in the sandy seabed.

Venomous spines on fins

Venomous tail spine

Deadly stone
The stonefish is a relative of the lionfish and it also lives in the tropics. It lies on the seabed and snatches any smaller fish that pass by. The stonefish has small spines that can inject a deadly venom. People sometimes die from treading on it by accident.

Sting in the tail
A stingray is named for the dagger-like venomous spines in its long tail. When it senses danger, it flicks its tail to attack.

41

Life in the dunes

When sand is dry, it is easily carried about by the wind. If the wind blows steadily from the sea to the land, it often pushes the sand into piles called sand dunes. Dunes have their own special wildlife. See the change as you walk inland from the sea.

Feeding by night
Snails that live on dunes feed mainly at night. During the day, they stay inside their shells to stop their bodies from drying out.

Feeding by day
You can often see sand lizards sunbathing before setting off to hunt. They get their energy from the warmth of the Sun. The lizards then scuttle over the sand in search of small insects.

Changing landscape
The part of the dune nearest the sea is usually made of bare, shifting sand. Further away from the sea, grasses begin to take root and they hold the sand grains together.

Sea lyme grass is a plant that can live on the seaward edge of dunes.

MAKING SAND MOVE

In this project, you can see how wind keeps sand grains on the move.

Hairdryer

1. Put a block of wood next to an empty ice-cube tray. Now make a small "dune" by piling sand onto the block.

2. Make a wind blow sideways across the "dune" either by blowing through a straw, or by holding a hairdryer close to the sand.

3. The sand in the "dune" will be carried sideways by the wind. The heaviest grains will not travel far, but lighter ones may reach the end of the tray.

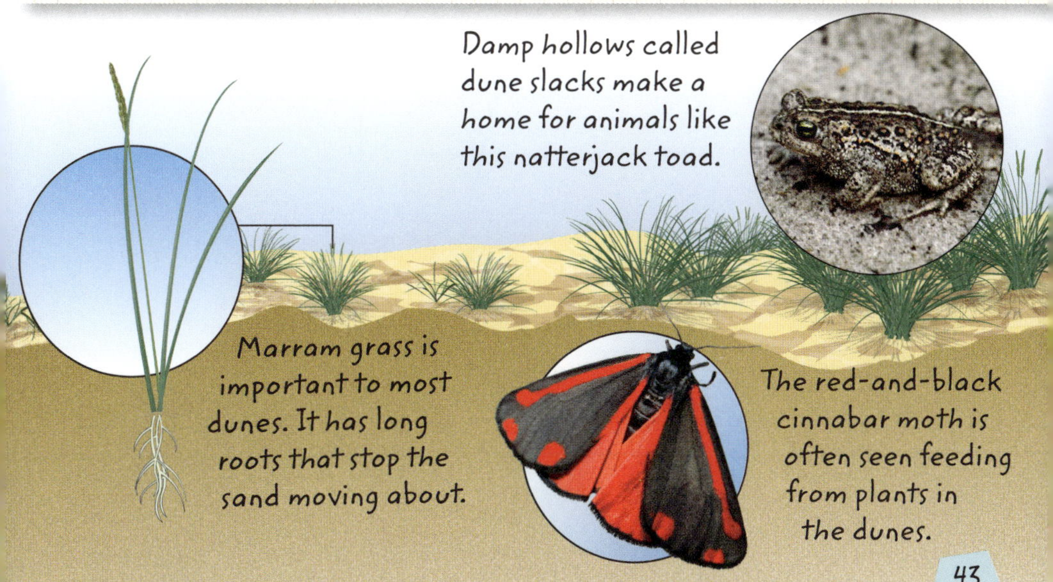

Damp hollows called dune slacks make a home for animals like this natterjack toad.

Marram grass is important to most dunes. It has long roots that stop the sand moving about.

The red-and-black cinnabar moth is often seen feeding from plants in the dunes.

43

Sandy shore

Sand is soft to walk on and it is easy to dig up and play with. Have you ever wondered exactly what sand is, or how it is made? To find out about sand, you will need to look very closely.

Glued by water

Sandcastles are made from millions of grains of damp sand. When you build a sandcastle, the water that surrounds each grain of sand works like glue and holds the sandcastle together. If the sand dries out, the castle soon falls down.

Volcanic sand

This sand is made from rock from a volcano. The sea grinds it down into a black sand.

Mineral sand

This forms when the sea grinds down solid rock. It contains silica, a substance used to make glass.

Shell sand

This sand is made from tiny pieces of shell. Damp shell sand sticks to skin, because most of it is flat.

MAKING A SAND TRAY

You can start your own sand collection by making this special cardboard tray. Let the sand dry out before you add it to your collection.

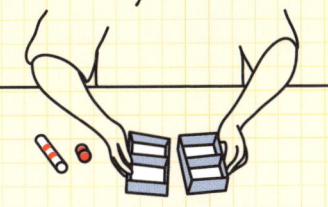

1. Glue four small cardboard boxes together, side-by-side.

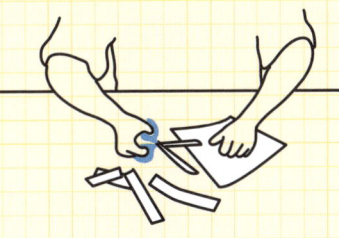

2. Carefully cut out cardboard for labels. Fold them in half and glue them to one wall of each section.

3. Now pour your sand into each section of the display case.

Fine-grained sand made of light-coloured rock

Fine-grained sand made of grey-layered rock

Very coarse sand made of volcanic rock

Coarse sand made of broken pieces of shell and coral

Jumping to safety

If you walk along a sandy beach, you may notice clouds of tiny animals jumping out of your way. These are sand hoppers — small relatives of shrimps and lobsters. They feed on rotting seaweed and jump by flicking their tails.

Coastal corals

Corals are small animals that often live close together. Many protect themselves by building hard cases. As the coral animals grow and then die, their cases pile up and can form huge banks called coral reefs.

Mushroom coral
This coral contains just one polyp (coral animal), protected by a stony cup that looks like part of a mushroom. It is not fixed to the seabed. If it is turned over, it can slowly pull itself the right way up.

Coming out to feed
These polyps are trailing their tentacles in the water to catch food. Their tentacles have tiny stinging threads that shoot out when a small animal brushes past them.

If a large animal comes close, the polyps quickly pull in their tentacles.

Cabbage coral

This cabbage coral looks very much like a plant, but each of its "leaves" is made up of hundreds of tiny coral animals living close together. Cabbage corals live near the surface, where the water is sometimes rough.

As cabbage corals grow and die, they help to build coral reefs.

Coral fans

Sea fans often grow in deep water and can be more than 3 m (10 ft) long. They do not have a hard casing and so can bend quite easily. Sea fans usually grow at right angles to the current. This gives them the best chance of catching any food that is drifting past. A large sea fan is often home to many other living things, including crabs, sponges, and barnacles.

The spreading shape of this purple sea fan shows that it is growing in calm water.

Shingle beach

Shingle beaches are made up of lots of small, rounded stones. They are quite difficult places for plants and animals to live in, as the sea keeps the stones on the move. A lot of the wildlife on a shingle beach lives high up on the shore, beyond the reach of the waves.

Searching for water

Shingle is full of air spaces and does not hold water. Plants that live on shingle need very long roots, so that they can reach the water far below the surface. They also need tough leaves, so they can cope with strong winds.

Sea holly has hard, prickly leaves.

Terns are small gulls.

Sea campion grows in round clumps.

The sea pea is one of the few plants that can live on open shingle banks.

Hidden on the beach

You might think that it is hard to hide on shingle. However, small birds like the ringed plover hide away by looking just like stones.

Disappearing eggs

Terns lay their eggs in hollows on a shingle bank. Their eggs are speckled, which makes them very hard to see against the surrounding stones.

A tern feeds by hovering above the water and then splashing down to catch small fish.

Tern's eggs

Oystercatchers are noisy birds with big beaks like hammers to smash open shells.

The yellow horned poppy grows seeds in a long pod.

Sanderling

Rock pipit

The ringed plover feeds close to the water.

Rocky shore

For many plants and animals, a rocky shore makes an ideal place to live. Unlike shingle, solid rock does not get dragged about by the waves. Small plants and animals can live on the rocks, without being battered to pieces or being swept away.

Layers of life

The best time to explore a rocky shore is at low tide. Some barnacles and winkles can survive out of water for a long time, so they can live high up on the rocks. Other sea animals, such as sea squirts and starfish, need to stay damp.

The turnstone scuttles over rocks, looking for small animals.

Lichens live on bare rock, just beyond the reach of waves. They grow very slowly, but live for a long time.

Sea squirts

Brittlestar

Life from long ago

Rocky shores can be very good places for fossil hunting. Fossils are the remains of plants or animals that have slowly turned to stone. This fossil is of an ammonite. Ammonites were common more than 66 million years ago.

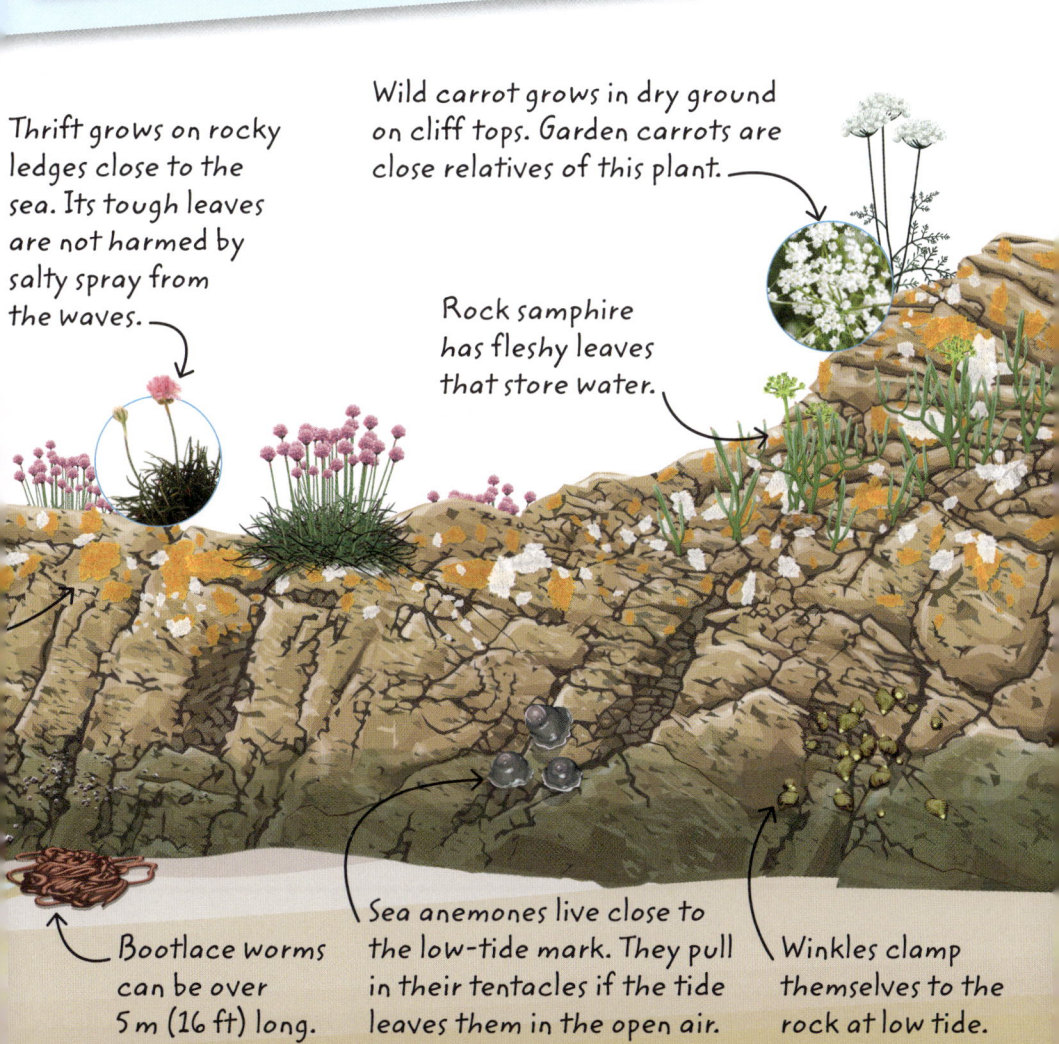

Thrift grows on rocky ledges close to the sea. Its tough leaves are not harmed by salty spray from the waves.

Wild carrot grows in dry ground on cliff tops. Garden carrots are close relatives of this plant.

Rock samphire has fleshy leaves that store water.

Bootlace worms can be over 5 m (16 ft) long.

Sea anemones live close to the low-tide mark. They pull in their tentacles if the tide leaves them in the open air.

Winkles clamp themselves to the rock at low tide.

Rock pool

When the tide falls, most of the shore is left high and dry. However, in a rock pool, some plants and animals can stay safely underwater until the sea returns. Every rock pool is different – shallow pools sometimes have only a few plants or animals, but deeper ones may be packed with life.

Toothed wrack

Water level at low tide

Winkle

Limpet

Closed beadlet anemone

Velvet swimming crab

Starfish

Open beadlet anemone

Sea urchin

MAKE A ROCK POOL VIEWER

Rock pools are fascinating places to explore. Ask an adult to help you make this rock pool viewer, so you can get a clear look at the animals in the pools without disturbing them.

1. Cut a piece of plastic tube about 10 cm (4 in) long. Trace around one end on a piece of clear plastic.

2. Cut out the plastic circle with scissors. Use sandpaper to sand the edges of the tube. Glue the piece of plastic to one end of the tube.

3. Once the glue has dried, your viewer is ready to use. Just push the plastic end into the water and have a look.

⚠️ Take care when visiting rock pools as wet rocks and seaweed can be very slippery. Also, watch out for the tide coming in!

Muddy shore and salt marsh

You won't find people lazing on a muddy beach, or soaking up the sunshine in a salt marsh. For some plants and animals, though, muddy shores are perfect places to live. Although the mud is salty, it is also rich in nutrients and full of life.

Glass from plants
Glasswort is a short, fleshy plant that lives close to the water's edge. Long ago, people collected glasswort and burned it, because its ashes can be used to make glass.

Glasswort has fat, rounded stems and tiny leaves.

Sea aster

Marsh flowers
Like many salt marsh plants, sea aster flowers quite late in summer. It grows away from the water's edge.

Seaside terrapin
Most terrapins live in fresh water, but the American diamondback lives in salty water near the coast. It feeds at night and often spends the day basking in the sunshine.

A painted lady butterfly drinks nectar from sea aster flowers.

Sea spurrey flowers close up quickly if the Sun goes in.

Sea purslane has small yellow flowers. It lives at the inland edge of salt marshes, where the ground is drier.

Teal fly over marshes in winter to look for food.

Lying in wait
A heron hunts by stealth. It wades into the water and then stands absolutely still. If a fish swims past, the heron stabs at it with its sharp beak.

Cord grass grows in wet, salty mud. It stops the mud being washed away and helps to turn it into dry land.

Sea plantain has narrow, leathery leaves and tiny flowers in long clusters.

Beauty in the marsh
Sea lavender has lots of small but brightly coloured flowers, and in late summer it often turns whole marshes purple. The flowers keep their colour if they are picked and allowed to dry out.

Mangrove swamp

In warm parts of the world, muddy coasts are often covered by mangrove trees. Their spreading roots stop the mud from being washed away. A mangrove swamp is a jungle that is flooded with seawater at high tide, and has its own special wildlife. Animals live in the mud, on the roots, and clamber among the branches.

Stick in the mud
Mangroves are unusual trees, because they can grow in salty water. They have special roots which anchor them in the mud and breathing roots that collect air.

Fish out of water
Mudskippers are finger-sized fish that can breathe air. They use their stumpy fins to climb up mangrove roots. When danger threatens, they hop back into the water.

Mudskipper clinging to a root.

Mangrove prop roots are anchored in mud.

Getting the message
At low tide tiny fiddler crabs come out of their mud burrows to search for food. Males have one especially large claw that they wave to attract a mate.

Spread out to dry
Anhingas, or snake birds, live in the swamps of the southern United States. They feed on fish and swim with just their heads and snake-like necks above the surface. After each fishing expedition, an anhinga spreads out its wings to dry.

Feathers dry in the sunshine.

Living on leaves
Mangrove leaves are tough and leathery, but for the proboscis monkey they are an important source of food. These rare monkeys live in mangrove swamps on the island of Borneo. Male proboscis monkeys are twice as big as the females and their noses are much larger.

Harbour and pier

A harbour is a busy place, where boats are tied up and where fish are brought to the shore. Harbour walls are usually made of rock, concrete, or wood. Below the high-tide mark, tiny plants and animals settle and soon it is full of life.

Keeping things clean

In busy harbours, the water can easily become polluted. This makes it difficult for sea animals to survive. If the water is clean, a harbour can be home to many different kinds of fish.

Many harbours have rivers flowing into them. Their water is less salty than water in the open sea.

Fighting for food

Gulls are nature's scavengers. They eat almost anything, from crabs and dead fish, to chips and sandwiches.

Sea slaters hide during the day. At night they look for scraps of food.

Top of the pile

Wooden pilings are home to many small animals and plants. At low tide some of these are easy to see.

Sea anemone

Mussels grow like bunches of grapes on wood or rocks.

Index

AB
ammonites 51
anhingas 57
arches 10

barnacles 25, 50
bees, cliff mining 20
birds 15, 16–17,
 20–21, 22
bladderwrack 19
blennies 28
boats, paper 13
bones 19
burrowers 26–27

C
camouflage 30–31
carrots, wild 51
cinnabar moths 43
cliffs 10, 11, 20–21
cod 36
conch shells 25
cone shells 18, 19, 24
corals 19, 40, 46–47
cord grass 55
cormorants 17, 21
cowries 24
crabs 8–9, 14, 31, 35,
 36, 38, 41, 52, 57
cuttlefish 39

D
diatoms 36
dogfish 34
dogs 16
dolphins 23
dragonets 29
driftwood 18
dunes 42–43

EF
eggs 21, 22, 23, 34,
 36, 49

fish 28–29, 30, 36,
 40–41
food 38–39
footprints 16–17
fossils 51

G
glasswort 54
gobies 29
gravity 14
grunions, California 23
guillemots 21
gulls 16, 20, 48, 59

HJK
harbours 58–59
herons 17, 55

jellyfish 37

kelps 32, 33, 37
kittiwakes 21

L
lichens 50
limpets 15, 25, 35, 52
lionfish 40
lizards, sand 42
lobsters 8, 45
lugworms 27

MNO
mangrove swamps
 56–57
marram grass 43
masks 31
molluscs 26, 27
mongoose, Asian 22
monkeys, proboscis 57
Moon 14
muddy shores 54–55,
 56
mudskippers 56
mussels 15, 59

notebooks 9

oarweed 14
octopuses 38, 39
olive shells 24
oystercatchers 15, 49

PR
pebbles 11
pelicans, brown 19
periwinkles 15
piddocks 26
pipefish 30
pipits, rock 15, 49
plankton 36
plants 14, 48, 51,
 54–55
Portuguese man-of-war
 39

prawns 15
puffins 21

rays 30, 41
rock pools 52–53
rocks 10–11, 44, 50–51

S
salt marshes 54–55
samphire, rock 51
sand 11, 16–17, 19, 42–43, 44–45
sand hoppers 45
sand masons 27
sandcastles 44
scallops 25
sea anemones 34, 51, 52, 59
sea aster 54
sea fans 47
sea lavender 55
sea lettuce 15, 33
sea lyme grass 42
sea plantain 55
sea purslane 55
sea squirts 39, 50
sea urchins 19, 26, 34, 52
seahorses 28
seals 23
seaweeds 19, 32–33, 35, 37
shells 18, 19, 24–25, 44
shingle 11, 48–49
shipworms 27
shore profiles 11, 15
skulls 19
snails 42
sole 30
stacks 10, 11
starfish 14, 18, 35, 50, 52
stingrays 41
stonefish 41
strandline 18
Sun 14, 55

T
terns 48, 49
terrapins 54
thrift 51
tidal zones 14–15
tides 14
toads, natterjack 43
topshells 15
tracks 16–17
turnstones 50
tusk shells 26

VW
venomous creatures 40–41
viewers, rock pool 53

waves 10, 12–13, 34, 50
weever fish 41
wind 12, 42, 43
winkles 50, 51, 52
worms 27, 51
wracks 32, 52
wrasses, cuckoo 29

Acknowledgements

Dorling Kindersley would like to thank:

Robin James and Mike Quarm from Weymouth Sealife Centre. Tina Robinson, Susan St. Louis, Shakera Mangera, Mark Haygarth, and Faith Nelson for design assistance. Gemma Ching-A-Sue and Alison Owen for modelling. Hilary Bird for indexing.

Starfish

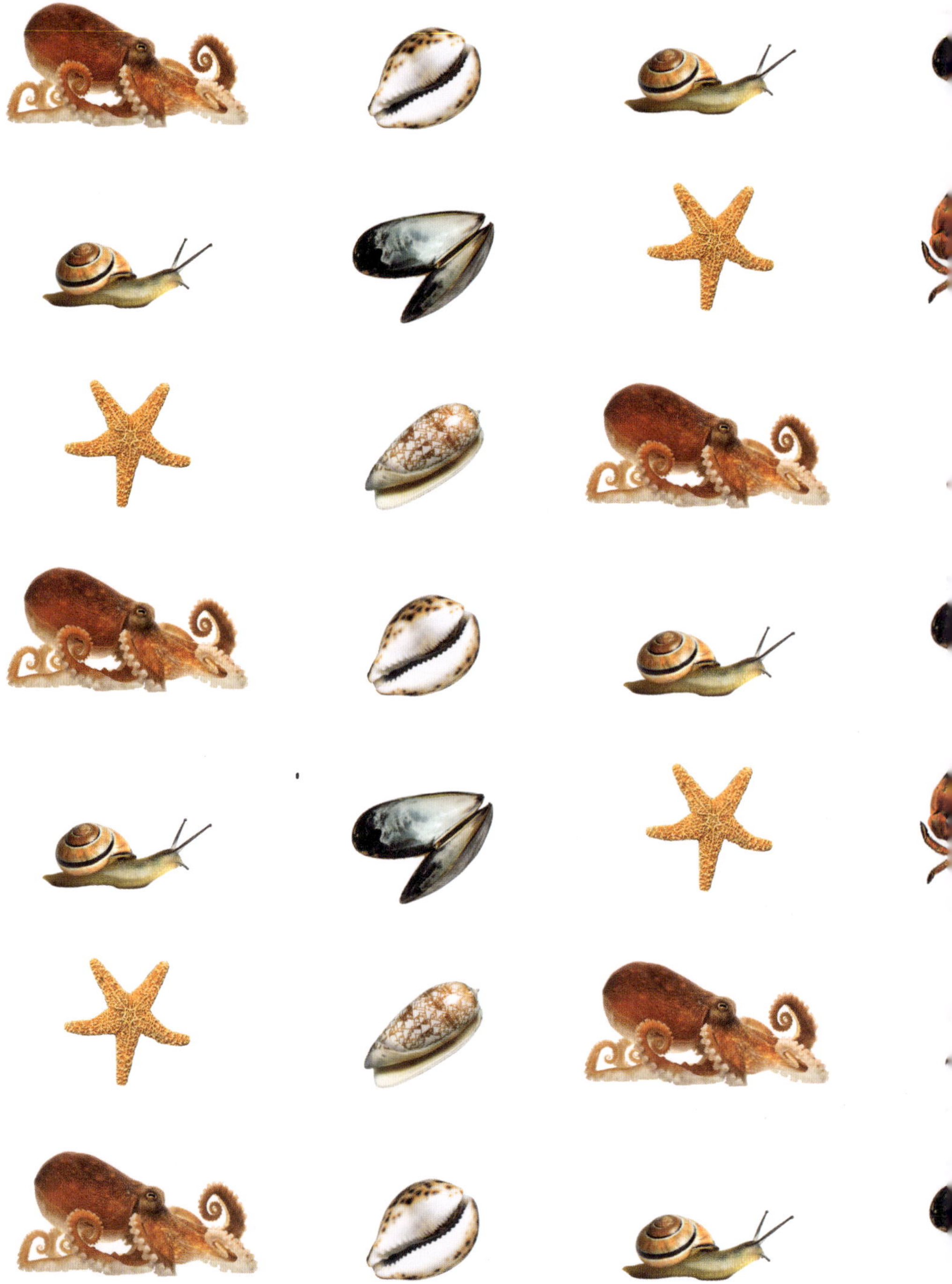

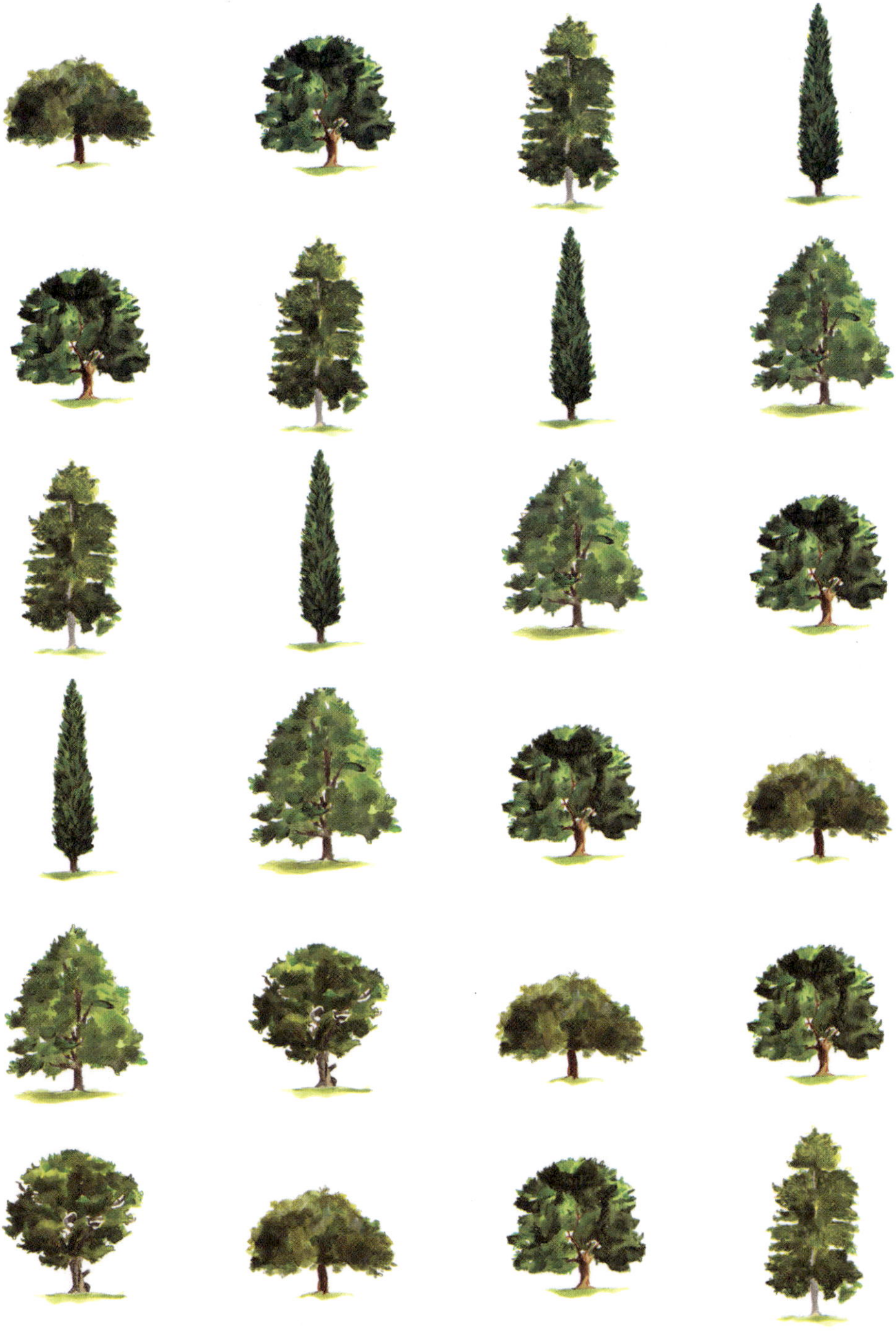

Deciduous tree leaves are green in summer.

Spruce needles have square sides.

The wake-robin is also called trillium.

Poison dart frogs live in the rainforest.

Jay feather

Acorns are a favourite food for squirrels.

Woodland and Forest

Written by Jamie Ambrose

Additional text: David Burnie and Linda Gamlin

DK

DK | Penguin Random House

Senior editor Gill Pitts
Editors Radhika Haswani, Olivia Stanford
Editorial assistance Cécile Landau
Senior art editor Ann Cannings
Art editor Kanika Kalra
Illustrators Abby Cook, Dan Crisp, Molly Lattin
Cartography co-ordinator Rajesh Mishra
Jacket co-ordinator Francesca Young
Jacket designers Dheeraj Arora, Amy Keast, Faith Nelson
DTP designers Syed Md. Farhan, Dheeraj Singh

Picture researcher Deepak Negi
Producer, pre-production Nadine King
Producer Isabell Schart
Managing editor Laura Gilbert
Deputy managing editor Vineetha Mokkil
Managing art editors Neha Ahuja Chowdhry, Diane Peyton Jones
Art director Martin Wilson
Publisher Sarah Larter
Publishing director Sophie Mitchell

First published in Great Britain in 2017 by
Dorling Kindersley Limited
80 Strand, London, WC2R 0RL

Copyright © 2017 Dorling Kindersley Limited
A Penguin Random House Company
8 7 6 5 4 3 2 1
001–308947–Nov/2017

All rights reserved.
No part of this publication may be reproduced, stored in or introduced into a retrieval system, or transmitted, in any form, or by any means (electronic, mechanical, photocopying, recording, or otherwise), without the prior written permission of the copyright owner.

A CIP catalogue record for this book is available from the British Library.
ISBN: 978-0-2412-8252-6

Printed and bound in China.

The publisher would like to thank the following for their kind permission to reproduce their photographs:
(Key: a-above; b-below/bottom; c-centre; f-far; l-left; r-right; t-top)

4 123RF.com: Michael Truchon (cr). **Dorling Kindersley**: Barnabas Kindersley (bl). **5 Alamy Stock Photo**: WILDLIFE GmbH (c). **7 iStockphoto.com**: Henk Bentlage (br). **8–9 iStockphoto.com**: IngaNielsen (Background). **8 iStockphoto.com**: Imgorthand (clb). **10 Fotolia**: Eric Isselee (cl). **12 123RF.com**: Filipe Frazao (cb). **13 Alamy Stock Photo**: Dinodia Photos (crb). **iStockphoto.com**: Guenter Guni (bl). **14 123RF.com**: dink101 (cl). **14–15 iStockphoto.com**: Oleksandr Smushko (c). **17 123RF.com**: Tamara Kulikova (cl). iStockphoto.com: PinkForest (crb). **18 Dorling Kindersley**: British Wildlife Centre, Surrey, UK (crb). **19 Getty Images**: Frank Pali (b). **20 Corbis**: Dieter Heinemann / Westend61 (tr). **21 Corbis**: Don Johnston / All Canada Photos (ca). **Dreamstime.com**: Mykola Ivashchenko (bl). **22 Alamy Stock Photo**: WILDLIFE GmbH (bc); Jixue Yang (tr). **23 Alamy Stock Photo**: Helene Rogers / Art Directors & TRIP (cb); Paul R. Sterry / Nature Photographers Ltd (ca). Corbis: Martin R‚gner / Westend61 (cr). **24 iStockphoto.com**: jax10289 (bl). **24–25 123RF.com**: Sonya Etchison (cb). **25 123RF.com**: Michael Truchon (ca). **26 Fotolia**: Eric Isselee (crb). **27 Dorling Kindersley**: British Wildlife Centre, Surrey, UK (tl). **iStockphoto.com**: Ivan Strba (r). **28 iStockphoto.com**: Atelopus (l); Guenter Guni (cr). **30 iStockphoto.com**: IMNATURE (c); mazzzur (br); servickuz (cl). **31 Alamy Stock Photo**: Klaus Ulrich Müller (cr). **SuperStock**: Josef Beck / imageBROKER (br). **32 iStockphoto.com**: Alatom (bl). **32–33 iStockphoto.com**: robas (c). **33 iStockphoto.com**: davidevison (crb). **35 Dorling Kindersley**: Barnabas Kindersley (c). **Dreamstime.com**: Alexander Pladdet (clb); Rudmer Zwerver (cb). iStockphoto.com: Saso Novoselic (br). **38 iStockphoto.com**: AustralianCamera (crb). **39 Getty Images**: Kathy Collins (l). **40 Alamy Stock Photo**: Buiten-Beeld / Hillebrand Breuker (cr). **iStockphoto.com**: Thomas Faull (clb). **41 iStockphoto.com**: Dennis Donohue (bl); GlobalP (cra). **45 123RF.com**: hxdyl (tl). **46 iStockphoto.com**: 4kodiak (cb). **47 Alamy Stock Photo**: Pulsar Images (crb). **48 iStockphoto.com**: Henk Bentlage (cr). **49 Alamy Stock Photo**: Kenneth Walters (tl). **iStockphoto.com**: USO (br). **50 Dreamstime.com**: Mrrgraz (clb). **iStockphoto.com**: Henkrik_L (cr); Paulina Lenting-Smulder (l). **52 iStockphoto.com**: Roger Rosentreter (cl). **52–53 iStockphoto.com**: Aleksandr_Gromov (b). **53 123RF.com**: anticiclo (cla). **54 Alamy Stock Photo**: Premaphotos (crb). **iStockphoto.com**: Jeff Goulden (cl).**55 123RF.com**: Diogo Baptista (b). **Alamy Stock Photo**: Design Pics Inc / Michael DeYoung (tl). **58 Alamy Stock Photo**: Edward Krupa (cra). **iStockphoto.com**: YinYang (clb). **59 iStockphoto.com**: Pierre-Yves Babelon (ca).

Cover images: Front: **Dreamstime.com**: Liligraphie bc; Back: **iStockphoto.com**: Ninell_Art tl

All other images © Dorling Kindersley
For further information see: www.dkimages.com

A WORLD OF IDEAS:
SEE ALL THERE IS TO KNOW
www.dk.com

Contents

- 8 Looking at forests
- 10 What is a forest?
- 12 Where are forests found?
- 14 Coniferous forests
- 16 Coniferous plants
- 18 Coniferous forest animals
- 20 Deciduous forests
- 22 Broad-leaved
- 24 Woodland flowers
- 26 Deciduous forest animals
- 28 Rainforests
- 30 Rainforest plants
- 32 Rainforest animals
- 34 Forest detective
- 36 How a forest forms
- 38 Changing seasons
- 40 Looking up
- 42 Life in a log
- 44 Why we need forests
- 46 Farming forests
- 48 Danger, keep clear!
- 50 Forest fungi
- 52 Forests in danger
- 54 Friends of the forest
- 56 Forest myths
- 58 Unusual forests
- 60 Index
- 61 Acknowledgements

Looking at forests

Trees may grow beside your home, or in a nearby park or square. However, while it's easy to look at a single tree, exploring a forest, where trees surround you, is different. These natural "living cities" will reveal their secrets – and inhabitants – more easily if you follow a few simple rules.

Make sure you dress for the outdoors. Wear warm, waterproof clothes if it is cold or wet.

No talking on the trail

For the best chance of seeing animals, keep as quiet as you can. Wild creatures don't like noise. Remember to stay on obvious paths or trails so you don't damage their habitat, or lose your way!

WHAT KIND OF TREE?

Trees come in all shapes and sizes. No two look exactly alike, but every tree's shape can help you identify what species it is. Here are some examples of common tree shapes.

CONICAL
Alder

GNARLED
Sessile oak

SPREADING
Hornbeam

BROAD
Beech

NARROW
Silver birch

COLUMNAR
Italian cypress

What is a forest?

A forest is a large area of land, so thickly covered by trees that little light reaches the ground. Different types of forest grow in different parts of the world. Forests provide food and shelter for many different animals.

Conifers such as the Norway spruce have green, needle-like leaves.

Look up! More animals live in forests than anywhere else on Earth. Many of them keep to the tops of trees. How many animals can you spot up there?

Coniferous forests
Coniferous forests contain tall, slender trees, such as pines or spruces, that make cones to produce seeds. They keep their needle-shaped leaves throughout the year.

Pine cones

This beech leaf is a typical wide and flat deciduous leaf.

Rainforest leaves come in all shapes and sizes.

Deciduous forests
The broader, spreading trees of deciduous forests have flat, green leaves in spring and summer that fall off in autumn. Trees such as beeches and oaks grow here.

Sweet chestnuts

Rainforests
Rainforests get lots of rain all year round. Some are so packed with different types of tree that raindrops take 10 minutes to reach the ground!

Red ginger flower

Where are forests found?

Forests cover about a third of the Earth's surface. As long as they get enough water, and temperatures are not too hot or too cold, they can grow almost anywhere. However, no matter where they are found, no two forests will look exactly the same.

- Rainforest
- Coniferous forest
- Deciduous forest

Amazon Rainforest, South America

This is the largest tropical rainforest on Earth, and more than half of it is found in Brazil. The Amazon Rainforest is so big that a fifth of all the world's bird species live here!

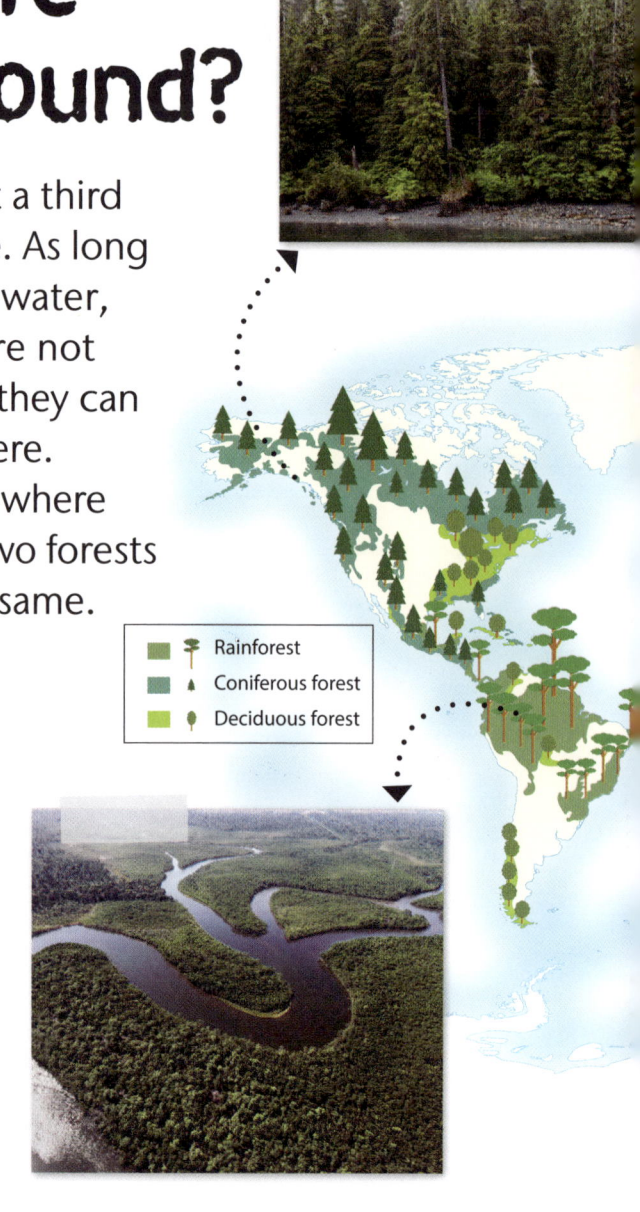

Tongass National Forest, Alaska
The largest national forest in the United States, Tongass is made up of spruce, hemlock, and cedar trees.

Black Forest, Germany
Germany's mountainous forest is called the "Black Forest" because the spruce trees grow so close together that parts of it are very dark to walk through!

Sundarbans, Asia
Mostly in Bangladesh, the Sundarbans is a mangrove forest. Mangrove trees grow well in wet, salty conditions, such as saltwater swamps.

Congo Rainforest, Africa
This rainforest is home to rare animals, such as lowland gorillas and forest elephants. Some parts are so dense, no one has ever seen them.

Coniferous forests

Most conifers are tough trees that can cope with extreme weather conditions. Their hard, needle-like leaves do not dry out as easily as the wide leaves of broad-leaved trees, so they do well in hot, dry climates, such as around the Mediterranean. They can also withstand cold, icy winters – the largest coniferous forests are in Russia and Canada.

Needle leaves

Many conifers, such as pine trees, have leaves that are shaped like needles. However, some conifers have leaves that are strap-like or scale-like. Almost all are thick, tough, and resinous.

Conifers grow tall and straight.

Sausage trees
Cones got their name because some, such as pine cones, are conical in shape. However, spruce cones are more like sausages, hanging down from the tree. Their needles also point downwards, helping them to shed snow.

Spruce needles have square sides.

Monkey puzzle
The monkey puzzle is an umbrella-shaped tree with sharply pointed leaves, which are arranged in a spiral. Also called the Chile pine, these trees are found in Chile and Argentina.

The leaf tips of monkey puzzle trees have sharp spines.

Conifers have flexible branches so that heavy snow and ice can slide off, which stops them from breaking.

TRACKING ANIMALS IN SNOW
Look for tracks in the snow — deer, crows, and squirrels live in the large coniferous forests of the north.

Deer | Crow | Squirrel (Front paw / Back paw)

Coniferous plants

Since conifers stay green all year, little sunlight reaches the forest floor. Also, conifer needles are acidic, like the juice of a lemon. When they break down they make the soil acidic too. The lack of light and acidic soil mean fewer plants grow here than elsewhere, but there are still many to spot.

Berry bearers
Scrambling plants, such as the blackberry, thrive in conifer forests. Their thorny vines allow them to climb up and over other plants towards the light, and the berries they produce provide food for animals and birds.

Blackberries make a tasty snack for foxes and deer.

Ferns
Ferns are flowerless plants, many of which love moist, shady conditions. This deer fern won't grow taller than 50 cm (20 in), but the giant chain fern, which grows underneath redwood trees, can be nearly 2 m (6.5 ft) tall!

Forest flowers provide nectar for passing insects.

Shrubs
You'll see few flowers in a coniferous forest, but some shrubs, such as wild roses, can bloom beneath the needles. They are found in the north of the United States, northern Europe, and Asia.

Lichens
Open conifer forests are home to lichens. These sponge-like growths are not plants, but are a partnership between an alga and a fungus. Reindeer lichen is a vital food for caribou in winter and can cover an entire forest floor.

Mosses
Mosses are simple plants known as bryophytes. They can't move water around their bodies, but instead soak it up like sponges. Like ferns, mosses produce no flowers. They release tiny spores to reproduce.

Coniferous forest animals

Many animals make their home in coniferous forests, especially in winter, when the trees provide shelter from snow. Some animals would not be able to live anywhere else, because they only eat things that live and grow in a coniferous forest.

Scots pine cones

Red squirrel

The crossbill uses its unique beak to tease out seeds from cones.

Cone specialists

Seeds from pine and other conifer cones are the main food for many birds, such as the crossbill, and small mammals. Some, such as squirrels, hide cones in secret larders to make sure they have enough food in winter.

Moose
The moose is the forest's largest grazing animal. In summer, it eats grass and other plants, but in winter it eats pine and spruce needles. Not many animals can do this!

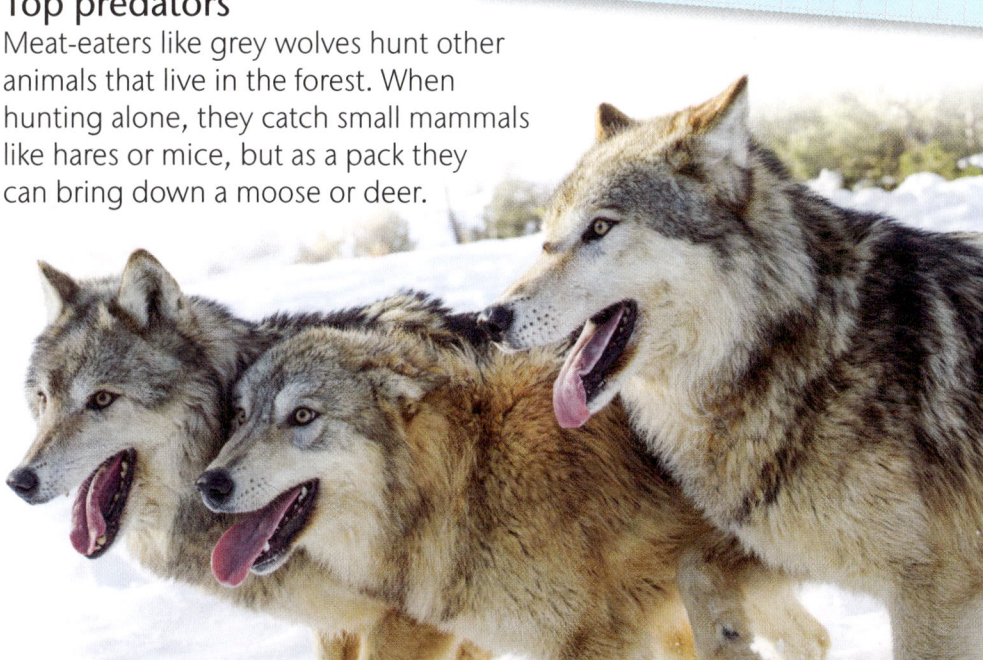

Top predators
Meat-eaters like grey wolves hunt other animals that live in the forest. When hunting alone, they catch small mammals like hares or mice, but as a pack they can bring down a moose or deer.

MAKE A CONE ANIMAL
How many animals can you create out of a spruce or pine cone? Start with this mouse...

To turn a pine cone into a mouse, use a couple of seeds or nuts for the ears.

Stick on a pair of toy eyes and add a piece of string for the tail.

Deciduous forests

In a deciduous forest, all or most of the trees lose their leaves when summer ends. Apart from a few evergreens, the trees shut down for the winter. When spring arrives, the Sun beams through to the forest floor until the trees have grown their new leaves. So in spring, flowers cover these forest floors like a carpet.

Sweet chestnut leaves

Long leaves
Sweet chestnut trees are easy to recognize. Their leaves are the longest in the forest and their bark often spirals round the trunk.

Winter leaves
Beech leaves are very smooth and shiny on top, with a wavy edge. Young beeches may keep their foliage in the winter, even though the leaves are dead and brown.

Beech leaves

Jagged edges
The basic shape of most oak leaves is the same, but their edges can be different. White oak leaves are jagged. In autumn, look for acorns that have fallen from the trees.

White oak leaves

Unlike deciduous trees, the leaves of coniferous trees stay green all year.

The leaves of deciduous trees may turn red, orange, or yellow.

Blazing forest
Some forests become a blaze of red and yellow just before the leaves fall. The most colourful displays are in the United States and Canada, because of the trees that grow there.

Look for worms, beetles, and many other animals living in the leaf litter.

Lovely litter
When leaves fall, they build up into leaf litter on the forest floor. Unlike man-made litter such as crisp packets, this litter will decompose (break down).

Dormice like to hide among dead leaves.

Broad-leaved

The leaves of broad-leaved trees come in many different shapes and sizes. They are called broad because they are thin, flat, and often wide. In North America and Europe, most broad-leaved trees are deciduous. In most other parts of the world, they are evergreen.

Lots of leaves
At the end of summer, many broad-leaved trees drop their leaves. Enough leaves may fall from one tree to make a heap 2 m (6.5 ft) high, which would cover you!

Broader leaves
Norway maples have leaves that are sometimes broader than they are long. Most maples have hand-shaped leaves. Stretch your fingers as wide as you can to see the basic shape.

Veins carry food and water around the leaf.

The pattern of the veins can help you identify a tree.

Stripy snake

Not all maple leaves are hand-shaped. This snakebark maple leaf is shaped like an arrowhead. Snakebark maples have stripy bark, so can you guess how they got their name?

This snakebark leaf has jagged edges and a pointed tip.

Leaves within leaves

Some leaves look as if they have been cut into smaller leaves with a pair of scissors. Ash trees have leaves like this. They are called compound leaves.

RUB A LEAF

You can make a record of vein patterns by laying a leaf from a broad-leaved tree upside down and putting paper over it. Rub the paper gently with a soft pencil and see the pattern appear. Remember to label your leaf rubbing when you have finished.

Woodland flowers

All plants need light to grow. However, woods are often quite dark. So how do woodland flowers manage to survive? In woods where the trees shed their leaves every year, many plants grow and flower in spring before the trees have grown new leaves.

Trees in bloom
Many trees, particularly those growing on the edge of a forest, produce flowers themselves in spring. Some, like these eastern redbuds, which are native to North America, are also planted in parks and gardens.

Wood anemone
Delicate, star-shaped wood anemones are one of the first flowers to appear on the forest floor in spring, particularly in older or ancient woodlands.

Wake-robin

The wake-robin is a woodland flower that grows mainly in North America and eastern Asia. Each flower has just three petals. The Native Americans who once lived in the woods made medicines from its fat underground roots.

Green sepals protect the flower as it grows.

The wake-robin is also called trillium.

The flower has three pointed petals.

Bluebells

Dazzling bluebells create a purple-blue haze in British woodlands in springtime. They are an important source of food for insects emerging after winter.

Food for all

Wild violets provide food for many creatures. Butterflies and tiny ants feed on their nectar, but other insects eat their leaves. Even deer and rabbits nibble their foliage, while mice and birds feast on their seeds.

Deciduous forest animals

A wide variety of creatures of all sizes live in deciduous forests. These range from tiny insects to huge grazing animals, such as deer, or even large black bears in North America. However, they all have to be able to adapt to the changing seasons in order to survive.

Birds
Birds of all types live in broadleaf forests. Most are easier to hear than to see, especially in spring, when they fill the forest with songs. Some, such as the tawny owl, sleep during the day, so they're almost impossible to spot.

Tawny owls hunt small mammals at night.

Grey squirrel

Squirrels
Unlike many mammals, squirrels don't sleep through the winter so they need to collect and store food for the colder months. Nuts keep well and squirrels collect them in autumn.

Red squirrel

Foxes

Foxes are common forest residents on many continents. These crafty predators hunt small mammals, such as rabbits, for food. They also eat berries, insects, reptiles, eggs, and food dropped or left by humans. They're not fussy!

Foxes have broad, bushy tails called brushes.

Deer

Deer are among the largest forest inhabitants. They eat new leaves and tree bark as well as grasses, shoots, and leaves. Woodlands provide shelter from the weather and hide them from predators, including human hunters.

Red deer are the largest land animals in the UK.

Creepy-crawlies

Earthworms, beetles, and woodlice eat leaves and rotting bark, turning them into rich soil. Spiders and centipedes hunt the leaf-eaters, while slugs and snails feed on all kinds of debris and forest fungi.

How many bugs can you spot on the forest floor?

Rainforests

Unlimited moisture and plenty of sunlight mean that trees can grow and grow – and that's exactly what happens in a tropical rainforest. The trees compete frantically with each other for the light, and reach tremendous heights as a result.

Teeming with life
Scientists think that over half of all the plant and animal species in the world, some not yet discovered, live in rainforest habitats. Many are found nowhere else on Earth.

Vital forests
Rainforests produce 20 per cent of the oxygen we need to breathe. They also absorb the greenhouse gas carbon dioxide, which helps control climate change and keeps the planet's weather stable.

Living layers
A tropical rainforest is like a tall building that has several different floors. Scientists call these "strata" or layers.

Emergents
Only the tallest trees, called "emergents", stick out of the highest layer.

Canopy
Usually between 20–40 m (65–130 ft) above ground, the canopy is hot and fairly dry. Most animals live here.

Understory
Shaded by the canopy, but still well above ground, this is the realm of ferns, vines, and smaller animals.

Shrub layer
As this layer is very dark, shorter plants and young trees compete to get the most sunlight.

Forest floor
The hottest, darkest, and dampest layer, the forest floor is covered with dead leaves and is alive with insects.

Rainforest plants

In tropical rainforests, where it is always wet and very warm, plants grow and flower all year round. Many different plants grow here, and some are very unusual, but all are specially adapted to their surroundings and could not grow in the wild anywhere else.

Amazing orchids

At least 10,000 different orchids grow in rainforests. Most get the water they need from moisture in the air, so they don't need soil to grow in. One of these, the vanilla orchid, is the source of the vanilla pods used to flavour ice cream!

The vanilla orchid has yellow flowers.

Orchids can be grown as houseplants.

Rafflesia smells so awful that it is also called the "corpse flower".

Giant parasite

Rafflesia has the largest single flower on Earth, growing to over 1 m (3 ft) across and weighing 11 kg (24 lb). This southeast Asian plant lives most of its life inside a vine, stealing food from a "host" plant, until it blooms.

Passionflower nectar is a favourite food for hummingbirds.

Hanging around

As vines, passionflowers climb up other plants and hang on by their curly tendrils. Bees and hummingbirds visit their flowers, but they must be quick because each blossom lasts for just a single day.

Poison dart frogs can be found in bromeliad "ponds".

Useful bromeliads

You already know one bromeliad – the pineapple – but these rainforest plants come in many varieties. They can grow on the ground, on rocks, or even on other plants. Their overlapping leaves hold rainwater, which provides a "pond" for insects and frogs high up in the trees.

Super lily

Each season, a giant water lily produces 40 to 50 leaves, but this is not why it is so special. A leaf of this South American rainforest plant can grow to more than 2.5 m (8 ft) across.

Rainforest animals

From mammals and birds to amphibians and insects, more animals live in rainforests than in any other habitat. Some of the largest are peaceful plant eaters, while the smallest may pack a deadly punch. Many of these animals blend in so well with their environment that they cannot be spotted easily.

Hidden hunter
The jaguar is one of the Amazon Rainforest's most secretive animals. It hunts at dusk or dawn, when its spotted coat provides the perfect camouflage. It even hunts in water, sometimes catching prey much bigger than itself.

Gardener of the forest
Wild orangutans are found on just two islands, Borneo and Sumatra, in Asia. Although highly endangered because of habitat loss, as fruit eaters, they help new trees to grow by spreading seeds around.

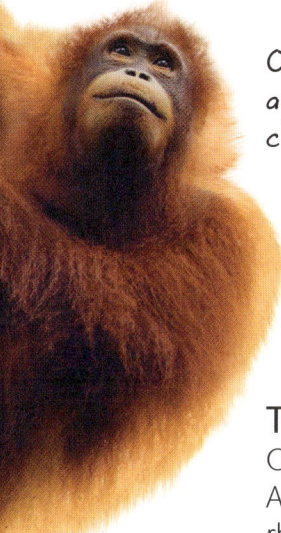

Orangutans are excellent climbers.

Out of the blue
With warm conditions and plenty of flowers, rainforests make ideal homes for butterflies. The metallic-looking blue morpho butterfly has a 13–20 cm (5–8 in) wingspan. It lives mainly in the canopy of Central and South American rainforests.

Treetop dweller
One of the strangest-looking Asian rainforest birds, the rhinoceros hornbill spends most of its time in treetops. Its horn-shaped beak acts like an amplifier, making its calls extra loud.

Small but deadly
The poison dart frog's bright colours warn predators to stay away. Some species of this Central and South American resident are so toxic that just licking its skin could be fatal to hungry hunters!

Forest detective

The next time you are out in a forest, see how many different things you can find. Start by looking carefully at your surroundings – binoculars and a magnifying glass can help here. Why not take a notebook and pencil along to write down any important observations?

Tree gall
Galls are grape-like growths on leaves, branches, or bark. Those made by insects, such as wasps, have a developing grub inside.

Open brown cones mean fine weather.

Closed green cones are not ripe yet!

Pine cones
Cones are nature's weather predictors. Open ones mean the air is dry and the weather should stay fine. Closed ones mean the air is moist and it might rain.

Owl pellet
A clump of fur and bones beneath a tree shows that an owl has roosted nearby. Soak the pellet in water and gently tease it apart with tweezers to find out what the owl has eaten.

These tiny mammal bones belong to a vole or mouse.

Jay feather
Discarded feathers tell you which birds are found in a forest. A bright-blue feather like this belongs to a jay. See what others you can find and identify.

Sycamore seeds
Winged seeds or "keys" on a woodland floor mean sycamores, ash, or maple trees are growing nearby. Try to match the seed to the tree.

Voles open nuts with their sharp teeth.

Hazelnuts
Where there are nuts, there are nut eaters. Look closely at holes in hazelnut or acorn shells to find teeth marks left by hungry voles, squirrels, or mice.

How a forest forms

A forest does not appear overnight. It takes years, sometimes centuries, before tiny seedlings grow into tall, majestic trees. Just like humans, a forest starts small, then grows and develops through many different stages. This is called "succession".

Events such as fires, storms, flooding, and logging can severely delay forest succession.

Bare ground
Everything starts with a firm base – in a forest's case, this means a patch of bare ground.

Herbs, grasses, and ferns
Bare ground is just what short, grassy plants like to grow in. Once grasses start to grow, tougher and taller plants such as herbs move in, and so do some ferns, such as bracken.

Shrubland
After several years, taller, thicker-stemmed shrubs start to grow. They crowd out the grasses and other plants. Some of these shrubs include small trees, which eventually grow taller than the rest of the plants.

SPOT AND LEARN
Plan a trip to a young forest or a mature forest with your friends and see how many different plants you can identify. Carry a notebook with you and write down your observations in it.

Young forest
After about 25 to 50 years, younger, faster-growing trees have taken over the site, shading out many of the smaller shrubs. The leaves they shed each year also change the nutrients in the soil.

Mature forest
After 50 to 150 years or so, what was once a young forest is now filled with bigger, sturdier trees. The canopy is thicker and fewer shrubs grow beneath it, unless some trees die or lose branches, letting in more light.

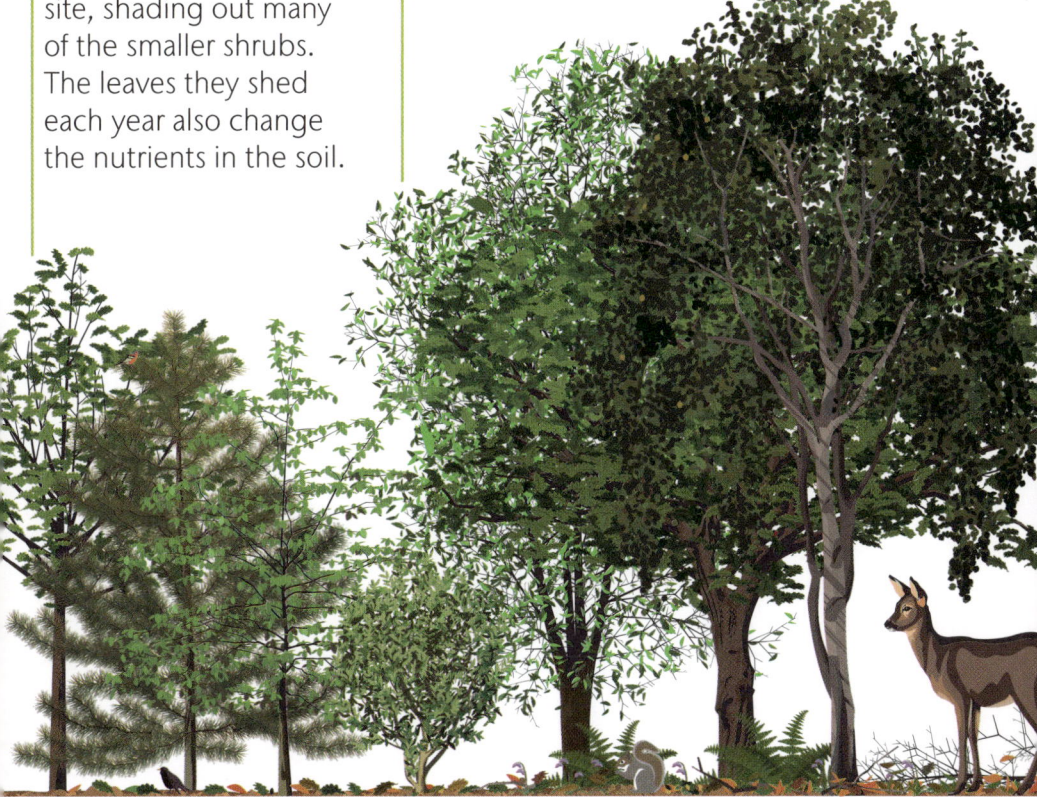

Changing seasons

In some parts of the world, there is a huge difference between the seasons – between summer and winter, or between the dry season and the rainy season. Trees have to adapt to the changing seasons as best they can. Some lose all their leaves in the winter or the dry season, while others shed just some of their leaves.

Small change

Forests near the equator – such as this rainforest in northeastern Australia – have just about the same climate all year round. The further you travel from the equator, the more the temperature changes between seasons.

KEEP A RECORD

Take a photo of your favourite tree at different times of the year, so you can see how its leaves grow and change.

Spring
In spring, deciduous trees produce new leaves. The leaves start their lives curled up inside buds, which expand quickly. The trees can then begin making food.

Summer
During summer, the leaves grow darker and tougher to keep hungry leaf-eating insects at bay. Some trees grow another set of leaves to replace those that have been eaten.

Autumn
A substance called chlorophyll makes leaves green. Before their leaves fall, trees break down their chlorophyll and the leaves may become red or yellow before finally turning brown.

Winter
The trees become dormant, which means they rest until spring, so their leaves are not needed to make food. During winter the branches are bare. New leaves will grow in spring and the cycle starts again.

Looking up

While some animals live among the roots and trunks of trees, many others go about their daily business high up in the branches. The next time you walk through a forest, don't forget to look up. There is a lot of life happening overhead!

Who lives where?
Many birds and mammals nest in holes in trees. In parts of Europe, you might see young, ferret-like pine martens peeking out of their cosy den. In spring you may spy a bird carrying nest materials, such as twigs or moss.

Hunt for hitchhikers
Mistletoe is a parasite that attaches itself to trees and takes nutrients from them. Its roots grow right into the wood of the host tree.

Mistletoe forms recognizable balls high up in tree branches.

What's moving?
The best way to observe a forest canopy is to lie down and look up. You might see squirrels high up in the trees, or even raccoons in a North American forest. In the rainforest, you may be lucky enough to spot a bright-red macaw.

Autumn harvest
In autumn, animals gather food to store for the winter. Some birds, such as the acorn woodpecker, drill holes in tree trunks to store acorns. Fewer leaves mean animals are easier to see, so look up to enjoy more than just the changing leaf colours.

NAME THAT BIRD
See how many different birds you can spot in the canopy. The best time to hear and see them is at dawn in spring, when males sing to attract females.

Life in a log

A fallen log might look dead, but in fact it is teeming with life. Home to all sorts of different tiny animals, plants, lichens, and fungi, logs also provide a safe place for seedlings to grow. This is why they are sometimes called "nurse logs".

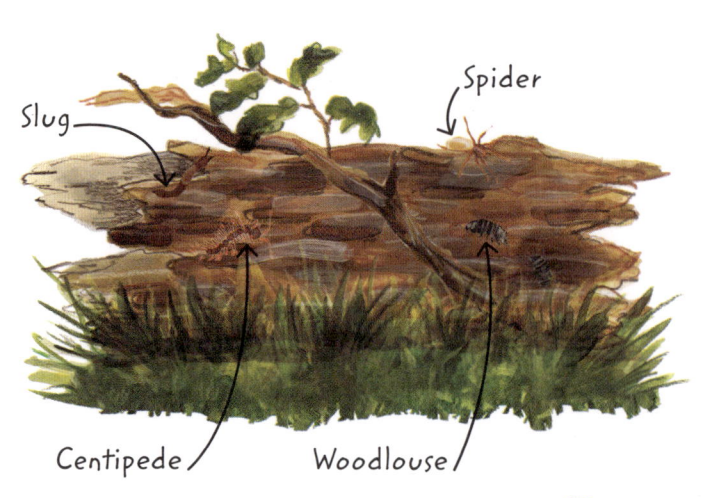

Newly fallen
Once a log falls, slugs and woodlice are among the first creatures to find shelter in the dark, moist places beneath it. They feed on decaying plants, and centipedes and spiders follow to eat them!

One year old
After one year, new creatures have moved in. Bark bugs live beneath the bark, while beetles drill holes to lay their eggs in. Their larvae eat the rotting wood. Mosses and fungi, such as ink cap mushrooms, appear on the log's surface.

Two years old

Full of holes and with crumbling bark, after two years the log is almost completely covered in lichens, fungi, and mosses. Wasps and stag beetles nest here, and woodpeckers come to feast on their grubs and larvae.

WHAT CAN YOU FIND?

If you find a fallen log, make a list of all the plants and animals you can see living on it. Return to the same log after some time has passed to see what changes have occurred.

Why we need forests

Besides providing homes and food for countless animals, trees supply us with a useful gift: wood. The first tools made by humans were probably sticks used for digging up roots. We still depend on wood and use it in dozens of different ways – to build houses, boats, furniture, toys, and much more!

Sap with a bounce
Rubber is the gummy sap that comes from rubber trees. It is collected by tapping – making cuts in the bark and gathering the sticky juice that flows out. This juice is then turned into rubber to make car and bicycle tyres, footballs, and rubber bands.

Crafty cork
Cork comes from the bark of the cork oak – a tree that grows around the Mediterranean. It is used for flooring, placemats, and champagne corks.

Festive favourite
In some countries, conifer trees are decorated for Christmas. These trees were originally cut down where they grew in forests. Today they are grown in specially planted Christmas-tree farms.

From pulp to paper

We make paper from wood. In factories called paper mills, tree trunks are ground up into pulp — a mushy substance that is then pressed, dried, dyed, and formed into paper products.

Paper is made in giant rolls in paper mills.

MAKING PAPER

You can recycle used paper to make new paper. To do this at home you will need newspaper, wire netting that an adult has nailed to a frame, a saucepan, and an old cloth or towel.

1. Shred clean newspaper into a saucepan of water. ASK AN ADULT to boil it until it turns into a mushy pulp.

2. When the pulp cools, pour it onto the wire netting. Let the water drain and turn the wet paper onto a clean cloth.

3. Once the pulp has become firm, hang the new paper up to dry.

You can decorate your new paper with petals or leaves.

Farming forests

Trees helped our ancestors to survive by providing them with food in the form of fruit and nuts. Much of the fruit we eat now has changed from the wild-grown food of our ancestors' day, because we grow it in artificial forests known as orchards. Some nuts and other foods, however, are still harvested from the wild.

Ancient apples
The ancestors of modern apples were tiny, sour-tasting crab apples. After thousands of years of selection by farmers, who chose trees with the largest, sweetest fruit, we now enjoy delicious apples from farmed trees.

Crab apples still grow in woodlands and hedgerows.

The world's favourite bean?
More than 2,000 years ago, people living in the rainforests of Central America discovered the fruit of the cocoa tree. Today this tree is grown around the world for its seeds, known as "beans". These are the source of all the world's chocolate!

Two from one

In Indonesia and the Caribbean, an evergreen called a nutmeg tree is grown in large plantations. Farmers harvest two spices from these trees. The seed is called nutmeg, while its lacy covering is known as mace. Both are ground up and used as spices.

Mace

Nutmeg

Wild and wonderful

Brazil-nut trees grow only in the rainforests of South America. They can be as tall as 60 m (200 ft), and are pollinated by just one species of wild rainforest bee. This means they aren't easy to grow in orchards.

Making nutshell boats

Make a nutshell boat by pressing a ball of sticky tac inside half a walnut shell. To make the sail, use a cocktail stick to pierce a leaf or piece of paper, being careful not to touch the sharp points. Push one end of the stick into the sticky tac and it is ready to go!

Danger, keep clear!

Most forest creatures are harmless, but some bite if they feel threatened, and others, like certain caterpillars, have stinging hairs on their bodies to ward off predators. Not all plants are human-friendly, either, so unless you are sure they won't bring you out in a rash – or worse – don't touch them.

Dangerous fungi

Bright colours are often nature's warning signals, so avoid touching any yellow or red fungi. Many mushrooms and toadstools contain toxic chemicals, which, if eaten, can kill you. Some are even deadly just to touch. The safest practice is to leave all fungi alone.

Biting bugs

Many insects have bites and stings. Spider bites can be painful, and some are even deadly. Some beetles can nip if picked up and ants, bees, and wasps can sting. Ticks are stealthy, and can bite you without you feeling it. Always check yourself over after a woodland walk for stowaways.

Plants to avoid

In North American forests, simply brushing against vines, such as poison ivy and poison oak, brings many people out in an itchy rash. In any forest, look out for stinging plants such as nettles, and plants with barbs or briars, such as wild roses. Never touch or eat any berries as they can be poisonous.

Poison ivy has glossy leaves.

⚠ Close encounters

Most animals will avoid humans if they hear you approach, but you may be lucky enough to see some up close. If you do, stay still and give them room and time to move away. Never run from a larger animal such as a bear. It may end up chasing you!

Respect snakes

Many snakes are harmless, and most simply want to avoid humans, but you may come across one on a walk that refuses to move. Keep away and walk around it if necessary, while admiring it from a safe distance.

Forest fungi

Scientists place fungi into a separate group – or "kingdom" – of living things because fungi are neither plants nor animals. The mushroom or toadstool you see is only a tiny part of a much bigger organism that is one of nature's great recyclers.

Beneficial bracket
A shelf-like growth on a tree is called a bracket fungus. Most bracket fungi appear only on dead or dying trees. Apart from breaking down rotting wood, they also provide food for other creatures.

Deadly destroyers
Some fungi harm forests. The honey fungus attacks trees underground, killing the roots of both conifers and deciduous trees. By the time mushrooms appear on their trunk, the trees are already doomed.

Dead-wood dweller
Golf ball-shaped fungi found on a rotting stump or fallen branch are most likely stump puffballs. When touched, the balls release clouds of tiny spores – each of which can become a new puffball fungus.

Underground arrangement

Fungi create a huge underground network called a mycelium, made up of fine threads called hyphae. The fly agaric toadstool's hyphae grow around a tree's roots. The hyphae take in sugar from the roots, but add nutrients and water to the soil to feed the tree.

⚠️ Warning: Don't touch any toadstools or fungi you find – they may be poisonous.

Look for fly agaric toadstools near birch and pine trees.

The mass of threads underground is the main part of the fungus.

Forests in danger

Forests have many natural enemies, such as plants or fungi that attack them, storms that destroy whole trees, or animals that eat tree bark or leaves. People can also hurt forests by starting forest fires, cutting down too many trees, or causing harmful pollution.

Fire hazards
Some fires are helpful – many plants need the heat they cause in order for their seeds to break open and grow. But unplanned fires destroy forests, damaging plants and harming animals.

Too much cutting
Every minute, we lose a forest the size of 20 football fields. Deforestation is caused when people cut down too many trees. This happens for many reasons, such as when people want more space to plant crops, graze cattle, or build towns.

Rain damage
Exhaust fumes from cars, and smoke from fires, factories, and power stations all release poisonous gases into the air. When they mix with water they fall as acid rain. If the rain is too acidic, trees lose their leaves and die.

Deadly fungi
Fungi that feed on wood are among a tree's greatest enemies. The fungi push tiny feeding threads into the wood, which can infect the tree.

Tree stranglers
Tropical strangler figs live up to their name! They wind around a tree, smothering its trunk and branches. The tree eventually dies.

HOW YOU CAN HELP
* Reduce, reuse, and recycle. By using recycled paper products, no new forests need to be cut down.
* Eat less meat from animals that require grazing land.
* Only buy wood from companies that source wood sustainably. They don't cut down too many trees and they also plant new ones.

Friends of the forest

A forest is home to many living things. Some animals feed on trees, but others protect them by eating their enemies. This is called "mutualism" because both the animals and the trees benefit from each other. Forests also benefit humans, who in turn can help protect these natural treasures.

Best bird friends
Forests offer birds safe places to nest as well as plenty of food. In return, birds like the chickadee eat the insects that nibble on tree leaves or suck sap. Other birds eat and scatter a tree's seeds so that new trees begin to grow.

Guarding ants
Whistling thorn acacia trees have special hollow spaces at the base of their spines where ants can nest. In return for their free homes, the ferocious stinging ants keep away leaf eaters, such as antelopes.

Wide-ranging rangers

Park rangers keep forests healthy and safe, by doing everything from planting new seedlings to removing diseased trees and getting rid of pests. Some national parks have junior ranger programmes, so you can take part in many forest-related activities.

Park rangers keep an eye out for forest fires.

Fighting fire

Teams of firefighters dig trenches, clear away debris, and pump water and chemicals to put out wildfires. Firefighters often start controlled fires to keep too many leaves and twigs from building up and fuelling a larger fire. Small fires also open up space for seedlings to grow.

Forest helper
You can be a friend to your local forest or woodland by picking up litter, being careful with campfires, and reporting damaged trees.

Forest myths

All over the world, people who live near forests have told tales of many strange and often wonderful creatures thought to inhabit them. From horned horses to trolls, giant ape-like creatures to tree spirits, woodlands have long been thought of as places of magic and mystery.

Horned horse
Stories of horses with a horn on their head that lived in forests have been told since ancient times. In Europe, they are called unicorns and were said to be pure white, gentle creatures, often with magical powers.

Tree-loving trolls
In northern Europe, the forests of Scandinavia are believed by some people to be the home of forest trolls. However, no one can agree exactly on what a troll looks like.

Forest spirits

The ancient Greeks believed forests were inhabited by spirits, which they called nymphs. Nymphs were said to be beautiful girls who lived near water, mountains, or woods. Wood or tree nymphs, called dryads, were even thought to live in or near particular trees.

Wild men of the woods

Many people in North America believe that huge, hairy, ape-like creatures still live deep in the woods of the USA and Canada. This beast has been called a "bigfoot", but it is also known as a "sasquatch" or even a "wood ape".

Tricksters in the trees

In North America, Native American tribes tell stories of "little spirits" that live in forests. They are called "canoti" by some tribes and are described as being tricksters who caused hunters to lose their way.

Unusual forests

Most people think of forests as lots of coniferous or deciduous trees growing over a large area, or even of rainforests, which contain a wider variety of trees. The Earth is full of forests that don't fit these descriptions. Many look strange or are unusual in other ways.

Forests of stone
The remains of ancient forests still exist. Prehistoric trees were buried under mud, ice, or ash due to volcanic explosions or floods. They have turned to stone over millions of years.

Forests of grass
In Southeast Asia, you can see forests filled with tall plants, but they aren't trees. These are bamboo forests, such as the one at Anji in China. Although it can grow very tall and strong, bamboo is actually a grass.

Forest of giants
New Zealand's Waipoua Forest has the greatest number of the planet's kauri trees. These conifers are among the oldest in the world. One of the largest kauris is also the oldest, and is thought to be about 2,000 years old.

Dry-climate forests
Dry-climate forest trees have special features to help them survive. Some, such as the African baobabs, store water in their trunks and limbs – they swell during the rainy season, saving water for later use.

Swamp forests
Swamps and riversides can be tough places for trees to grow, as their roots need to breathe. Many trees, such as mangroves, arch their roots above the water's surface so that they can take in lots of air.

Index

A
acid rain 53
alders 9
Amazon Rainforest 12, 32
ants 48, 54
apples 46
ashes 23, 35

B
bamboo 58
baobab trees 59
bears 26, 49
beeches 9, 11, 20
beetles 21, 27, 42, 43, 48
berries 16, 27, 49
bigfoot 57
birds 16, 18, 26, 31, 33, 35, 40–41, 54
Black Forest 13
bluebells 25
Brazil nuts 47
broad-leaved trees 14, 22–23
butterflies 25, 33

C
canopy 29, 37, 41
canoti 57
chestnuts, sweet 11, 20
Christmas trees 44
cocoa beans 46
cones 10, 15, 18–19, 34
Congo Rainforest 13
coniferous forests 10, 14–19
cork 44
crossbills 18
cypresses, Italian 9

D
deciduous forests 11, 20–27, 38–39
deer 15, 16, 19, 25, 26, 27
deforestation 52
dry-climate forests 59

EF
evergreens 20, 22

farming forests 46–47
feathers 35
ferns 16, 29, 36
flowers 24–25, 30–31
food 46–47
forest fires 52, 55
formation of forests 36–37
foxes 16, 27
frogs 31, 33
fruit 46
fungi 42–43, 48, 50–51, 53

GH
grasses 27, 36, 58

hornbeams 9
hornbills, rhinoceros 33
hummingbirds 31

IJKL
insects 17, 25, 27, 29, 31, 32, 34, 39, 48, 54

jaguars 32

kauri trees 59

leaves 10–11, 14–15, 20–23, 34, 37–39
leaf rubbing 23
lichens 17, 42, 43
logs 42–43

M
mangroves 13, 59
maples 22, 23, 35
mistletoe 40
monkey puzzle trees 15
moose 19
mosses 17, 42, 43
myths 56–57

N
needles, conifer 10, 14, 15, 16
nests 40, 43, 54
nutmeg 47
nuts 19, 26, 35, 46–47
nutshell boats 47
nymphs 57

O
oaks 9, 11, 20, 44
orangutans 33
orchids 30
owls 26, 35

P

paper 45
passionflowers 31
pellets, owl 35
pine martens 40
pine trees 10,
  14, 15, 18, 19
plants 16–17, 19, 24,
  28–31, 36–37, 49, 58
poison 31, 33, 48–49

R

rafflesia 30
rainforests 11–13,
  28–33
rangers 55
redbuds, eastern 24
redwood trees 16
rubber 44

S

seasons 26, 38–39
seeds 10, 18, 25, 33,
  35, 52, 54
silver birches 9
snakes 49
spruce trees 10, 13, 15
squirrels 15, 18, 26, 35
strangler figs 53
succession 36–37
Sundarbans 13
sycamores 35

T

toadstools 48, 50–51
Tongass National
  Forest 13
trolls 56

UVW

unicorns 56

violets 25
voles 35

wake-robins 25
water lilies 31
wolves 19
wood 40, 42, 44–45,
  50, 53
wood anemones 24
woodpeckers 41, 43

Acknowledgements

**Dorling Kindersley
would like to thank:**

Hilary Bird for indexing.
Kathleen Teece for
editorial assistance.
Faith Nelson for
design assistance.

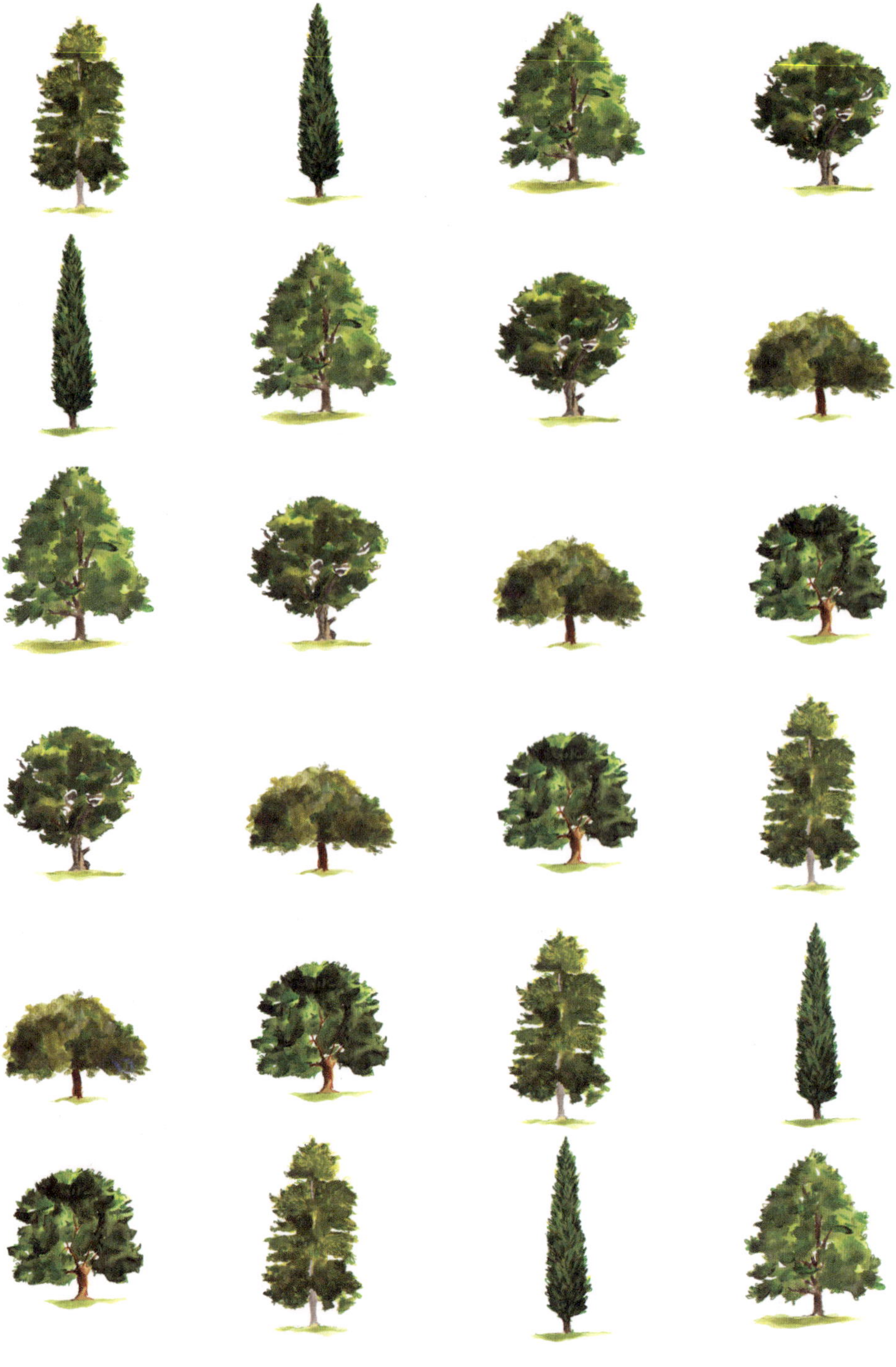